T0196485

REAL EXPERIENCES. REAL PAIN.

WHEN LIFE HURTS

AMBER SIRSTAD, MA

WESTBOW
PRESS®
A DIVISION OF THOMAS NELSON
& ZONDERVAN

WestBow Press books may be ordered through booksellers or by contacting:

WestBow Press
A Division of Thomas Nelson & Zondervan
1663 Liberty Drive
Bloomington, IN 47403
www.westbowpress.com
1 (866) 928-1240

ISBN: 978-1-5127-6563-2 (sc)
ISBN: 978-1-5127-6564-9 (hc)
ISBN: 978-1-5127-6562-5 (e)

Library of Congress Control Number: 2016919470

Print information available on the last page.

WestBow Press rev. date: 12/08/2016

TABLE OF CONTENTS

FOREWORD

I am honored to respond to Amber Sirstad's invitation to introduce you to her book, *When Life Hurts: Real Experiences. Real Pain.* I have known Amber the past two years as a graduate student in Corban University's clinical mental health counseling program, where I served as her faculty instructor and advisor. We have held many discussions about her trials and triumphs with pain and suffering and how God has always been at her side through it all. Though our time together has been brief, it has been an incredible joy to work with Amber, who brings optimism, humility, and delightful enthusiasm to those in her circle of influence. Her book will most certainly enlarge this circle by encouraging many others with clues on navigating survivorship in the midst of the storms of life.

Amber, a 26-year-old author, recorded musician, and, most recently, mental health counselor graduate, writes from the heart with poignant honesty and a twist of humor. Her life stories include living with two potentially fatal diseases that will grab your attention and cause you to dig deep and to reflect upon your own life challenges. She shares her personal thoughts on the gnawing question of why she has to suffer such significant medical problems at such a young age with many dreams yet to accomplish. Amber describes her deep convictions and personal relationship with Jesus, her anchor who has provided peace and strength in the midst of her life's storms. She sprinkles in short stories of close friends' painful life and death journeys, painting a broader landscape of human survivorship.

Amber's concluding thoughts in *When Life Hurts: Real Experiences.*

Real Pain suggest that through perseverance, dedication, and hard work, you can chase after your dreams and even fulfill them when you invite God to be involved. Sit in a favorite chair with your cup of coffee or sweet tea while you step into Amber's journey full of surprises, laughter, and tears, and experience her encouragement as you discover you are not alone in your suffering.

Linda Uhl Keller, PhD.
Associate Professor
Clinical Mental Health Counseling Program
Corban University

INTRODUCTION

Everyone experiences pain to some magnitude. We are just like everyone else...until *it* happens to us. Of course we, as humans, have the tendency to compare ourselves amongst ourselves. We don't like to feel sorry for ourselves because our brother or sister next to us is seemingly going through something much worse. However, with that mindset, we can't fully heal from our emotional and mental wounds. It's okay to admit that you are in pain. It's okay to admit that you have those days when it *appears* as though everything that could go wrong went wrong.

If at any time, while reading this book, an experience or memory comes to the forefront of your mind, I encourage you to write it down. And who knows, you might see that you have the makings of a wonderful book that can help others who are experiencing real hurt.

I have heard of life being compared to a roller coaster. It starts out slow and picks up momentum. There are ups and downs. There are times when you feel like everything has just been flipped upside down. There are times when you can't stop laughing and then there are times when you feel as though your heart is quickly being pulled out of your chest. Or what about life being compared to a tornado? Tornados are known to cause mass destruction. You can't control what a tornado does. When crisis happens, life seems like mass chaos. You have no control. Life as you know it becomes completely...messy. Those are the times that I want to talk about—the times when it feels like you have been stabbed in the heart with a twelve-inch blade... the times when life hurts.

DEDICATIONS

God—For giving me the strength to pursue my dreams and for
being my Rock that I so desperately need. Dr. Keller—
For your support and willingness to help in whatever way you
could. Corban Family—For showing me the true meaning
of empathy. Contributors—For reaching deep down into the
secret places of your heart and sharing with the
world part of your pain and suffering.

Chapter 1

EXPECTING THE UNEXPECTED

One can never consent to creep when one feels an impulse to soar.
—Helen Keller

It was an early summer morning in the beginning of August 2009. The weather was beautiful...that is if you were fortunate to have air conditioning. I woke up on Saturday morning, not knowing how my life would change. I made my way to my father's office as I had this deep intense theological question I wanted to ask him. I sat down for about ten minutes not saying a word. I finally posed the question that had been percolating through my mind for quite some time. I asked, "Dad, how on earth am I supposed to speak at Ladies Conferences if I don't have any stories?!" At that point my main story was that I came from a home where my parents were divorced. I also was diagnosed with asthma when I was two years old and have struggled with my breathing ever since. I can't just go around and tell the same stories all of the time. His answer was not as deep as I had anticipated. His reply was, "Well...I suppose you could always ask God to give you stories." Wow. I never thought of that. What a great but simple idea.

I sat for another five minutes in complete silence. I made my way back to my bedroom to get ready for the day. I said a very simple, quick, 10-second prayer, "God, please give me some stories so I can be able to relate better to people. Please and thanks." I am thankful that God hears our simple prayers. But I wish that He skipped over our un-thought-through prayers at times. However, He doesn't.

Thirty minutes later I got in my car and headed north towards the freeway. Once I was on the freeway, I immediately went into the left lane. I had the windows down and the music blaring. The song that was playing was "You Are My Hiding Place" by the Christian music group Selah. I was going about seventy miles per hour, and all of the sudden something very unexpected happened.

My hood flew up and slammed against my windshield. For about two seconds, everything stopped.

What in the world just happened!?

I was brought back to reality when it hit me that I had lost all visual. The impact of the slam had turned my rear view mirror as well as my two side mirrors. I could see nothing except the color of my hood that blanketed my entire windshield.

When tragedy hits, it feels as though we can't see anything around us. The only thing that we can see is what is right in front of our face, blinded by a solid windowless curtain. Pain. Crisis. Heartache. Hurt.

My first physical reaction was rolling my eyes and sighing *very* loudly. I don't have luck with cars—at all. And so I was irritated because now my hood was completely messed up. Instead of slamming on my brakes quickly, I slowly pressed on the brakes and pulled over to the left shoulder. All I know is that it was the Lord who protected me. I couldn't see where the lane in front of me was going when I was still driving, nor could I see if there were any cars beside me, in front of me, or behind me.

Finally, I was safe on the side of the road. My hands were gripping the steering wheel with extreme tension. My windshield was cracked right down the middle. My first thought was, "If I move, then the windshield is going to shatter into a million pieces." I sat still—very still. I finally realized that I had to do something and I couldn't sit there all day. I took a deep breath and started to move. One knuckle at a time.

Sometimes when we go through crisis, it isn't the quantity that matters, per se, but the quality. It's not that we have to continue to be on the go and do a million things, but it's the fact that we keep doing *something*. Even if that something is just being able to breathe. Just keep breathing. Just keep waking up every day. Even if that is all you can do, one minute at a time.

I finally was able to remove one hand from the steering wheel. I put my right hand on my lap and continued to take deep breaths. Once I realized everything was okay, I slowly turned off the music and put my car in park. Phew. The hardest part was over. But what do I do now? I slowly opened the door and was *sure* that my car was going to fall into a million pieces on the side of the highway. However, it didn't, and that made me happy. I retrieved my cell phone and got out of my car. I tried to pull my hood back, but it wouldn't budge—at all. Great. *Just what I need. A poor college student with a stack of medical bills, a part time minimum wage job, and now I am going to have to get a new car.*

I sat in amazement for a few minutes realizing that I could have been in a horrible car accident, creamed by other vehicles around me. But I wasn't. Thank God, for He provided sight in my blindness.

I called my father, not knowing what else to do. Once he picked up, I said, "Hi Dad! So. What are you up to?! Nothing? Oh great! My hood just flew up and I am sitting on the side of I-84 and it won't go down and I don't know what to do." He noted that he would be there in twenty minutes. So I had twenty minutes to sit on the freeway. What to do?! Why not take a nap? I lay down in the back with my legs hanging out. I closed my eyes hoping to sleep for a few minutes. I heard a car pull up and thought it was my father. I opened my eyes and a police officer was standing *right* in front of me.

I don't think I have ever moved so quickly in my life. After realizing everything was okay and everyone was safe, the officer left. A short while later my father pulled up. He got out of his car, walked over, looked at me, looked at the hood, and looked back up at me. His first remarks were words that, once they sank into my late-teen thick skull, would forever change my life. If you know my father, the visual is what makes the story. In his deep monotone voice, he said, "Well, you asked God for stories." That's all he said. There was no asking me if I was okay or asking me if everything was alright. There was no calming my intense irritation for an even more defected vehicle than it already was. He simply stated the obvious...that our God does hear our prayers—no matter how simple they are.

The psalmist David and I have had *many* agreements, and many similar conversations and prayers to God. I often compare him to females with their wavering emotions—up and down, up and down. But even though it appears as though David was very fickle, he was also a man after God's own heart. So that leaves hope for the rest of us! He said something that leaves me in awe every time I read, quote, or hear it.

> When I consider thy heavens, the work of thy fingers, the moon and the stars, which thou hast ordained; What is man, that thou art mindful of him? And the son of man, that thou visitest him?
>
> —Psalms 8:3-4

Wow. He knew exactly where I was at approximately 10:48 a.m. on that Saturday morning. He knew what was going to happen to my car. He knew that I wasn't going to be able to see *anything*. He knew and He cared.

God created the whole entire universe. God created the rolling hills, the roaring rivers, and the wide oceans. But that's not all He created. He also created the dry deserts and the dark valleys. That's right. The dark valleys. The same God who created the tallest mountain in the world also created the lowest valley in the world.

CHAPTER 2

SEIZE THE DAY

*Pain is temporary. It may last a minute, or an hour, or
a year, but eventually it will subside and something else
will take its place. If I quit, however, it lasts forever.*
—Lance Armstrong.

ife can sometimes seem rather confusing. I'm sure most of
us have all been there at one point in our life. Everything
is going perfectly and almost as planned and then out of
the blue...BAM! Life happens. So what do we do? Good question.
Unfortunately, if you're looking for a deep intellectual answer, then
you should probably just stop reading. The only answer that I have is:
just keep going. But I guess that actually could be considered a deep
intellectual answer, depending on how you read into it.

It was May 11, 2001, which landed on a Saturday. I had to wake
up at 4:30 a.m. because I and a group of friends from my local church
were going to pile into a twelve-passenger van and head about three
hours east to La Grande, OR. We were scheduled to attend one of my
last Jr. Bible Quizzing tournaments. I had put in an endless number
of hours memorizing portions of the New Testament. I remember
literally jumping out of bed because I was so excited.

We left Hood River and stopped at McDonald's in The Dalles. I remember eating a sausage McMuffin and drinking a Dr. Pepper. So far so good! We got on the road and we were headed to La Grande. I was sitting in the very back along with three other girls. About twenty minutes east of The Dalles, I decided to take a nap. I knew I had a long day in front of me, and so I leaned up against the window and closed my eyes. What happened next was definitely unexpected.

I remember it like it was yesterday. The details have been forever ingrained in my memory. The brain is a fascinating organ. However, at times it can be tricky. Things that I want to remember, I generally don't. Likewise, things I don't want to remember, I generally do.

I woke up and immediately yelled in my mind out of fear, "God! I'm too young to die!" I knew I was going to die. I kept on thinking that this was never how I imagined death. Even as an 11-year-old child, I had thought about death and dying many times—never like that. It was...surreal.

I had absolutely no control over my body. I was in fact having a grand mal seizure. Of course I didn't know what it was at that moment. My eyes were rolling back and forth. My whole body was jerking. I was drooling down the side of my mouth. Everything felt so...foreign. I had no control...except for my mind. The only thing I could control was what I was thinking.

When we are abruptly thrown right into the middle of a crisis situation, more times than not we can't really control what is going on externally. If we could, then we would probably never experience a crisis. But what we can control is what goes on internally in our mind. If you could read and close your eyes at the same time, I would have you do a small exercise, but since you can't then we will just pretend. Imagine you are standing on the free throw line on the basketball court. The stadium is crowded with people cheering your name. You dribble the ball several times. You look back and forth intently at the basketball and then the hoop. You drown out everybody else and it is just you, the ball, and the hoop. You take the shot. Did you make it? Or did you miss it? Chances are you probably not only made it, but that it was a swish! This just goes to show that we can indeed control our thoughts.

Every time my eyes would roll forward I would make eye contact with the person in front of me. The girl that was sitting in front of me was turned around just staring. I remember trying to scream as loud as I could, but nothing was coming out. I felt utterly and completely helpless. Nobody was noticing me in my worst condition ever. I just knew that I was going to die. But then something came over me. Or should I say Someone. I knew that if I was going to live that I had to get one of the girl's attention.

I counted to three in my mind and with all of my strength I tried to hit the girl next to me to get her attention. What I thought was going to be a very intense punch ended up being a small tap. They briefly looked over at me and told me to knock it off. Apparently, they thought that I was just being "Amber" and goofing around. All of that energy went to nothing. Great. So I knew I had to do it again. I counted to three and did the exact same thing. This time I had different results. They looked over at me again and said for me to stop it. But they noticed the drool, and I *never* drool.

Score. I knew I was going to be okay. One of the girls got my sister, Krystal's, attention. She turned around and saw me. Immediately she knew I was having a seizure. I remember the driver pulling over and calmly calling 911. Krystal came back to me and was talking to me while all of the other girls were seemingly having meltdowns. She reached in my mouth (probably not the smartest idea) and pulled my tongue out so I didn't choke on it. I remember her praying in between the moments where she was encouraging me that everything was going to be okay. Even at this time I was sure that I was on my death bed.

We pulled over on the side of the road right next to...the middle of nowhere. We stopped about 15 miles west of Boardman, Oregon...

which is also in the middle of nowhere. I was feeling very fidgety and wanted to get out of the van...now! We pulled over and I got out. I had to get fresh air. I had to walk. I had to do...something. Anything.

One of the scariest parts of the whole ordeal was when I started to talk (I know, I just set myself up for criticism). What I was thinking was not what was coming out. I remember thinking, "Oh my word. I am never going to be able to talk again." It was just noise. I kept on trying to talk but nothing would make sense. It took close to 15 minutes for me to start making sense. Slowly things started coming together. I finally realized that I might not be dying as much as it seemed like I was.

The first responder was an off-duty EMT. He pulled up with his baby girl in the back seat. A few minutes later the ambulance showed up with two other paramedics. They put a warm blanket on my lap and started to take my vitals. They were trying to decide if I should go in the ambulance or if I would be okay staying in the van. They basically left the decision up to me, so clearly I decided to stay in the van. The next choice to make was if we were to go back home or head on to La Grande. It was suggested that we just head back home. And so that is what we did.

For the next three days I did not sleep at all. I refused to go to sleep. I thought that it was sleeping that caused my seizure. I went to the hospital to get a CAT scan the next week. My father begged the doctor to tell me that sleeping isn't what caused the seizure, and the doctor assured me that sleeping is what would be best for me. I was skeptical at first but decided to trust him.

We were to go back to the hospital three days after the CAT scan was conducted to get the results. I remember it like it was yesterday. Here I was, eleven years old and scared out of my mind. I had been to the hospital many times, but never for a reason that was focused on my brain. I was sitting in the exam room behind the door. I was patiently waiting for the doctor with my father in the room. I had no idea what to expect. At that time, I didn't know much about Google, so I didn't know all the different reasons why a person could have a seizure. I am sure if I did know about Google, then I would have self-diagnosed myself with an incurable disease that says I would be dead within the week.

We were sitting there quietly and I was wringing my hands together. Waiting. The door swung open and my doctor made a grand entrance with a huge smile on his face and loudly proclaimed, "There is nothing wrong!" Nothing wrong?! You mean I am going to live?! What a relief! He didn't really understand why it happened, but he knew that there was no visible reason that showed in the scans. Up until that point, I had not had a good night of sleep. When I had my seizure I was sleeping; therefore, I thought that if I fell asleep again I would have another seizure—basic textbook conditioning. The only instructions were to go home and sleep! Obviously, we knew to keep an eye out for specific signs, but other than that I was cleared to resume life and go back to normal.

I immediately started to re-plan out my whole entire life. Five minutes prior, I thought that I was going to have to go home and pick out what I wanted to wear to my own funeral. Now I had my whole life in front of me! The opportunities were endless!

Chapter 3

THE VALLEY OF BACA

Blessed is the man whose strength is in thee; in whose heart are
the ways of them. Who passing through the valley of Baca make
it a well; the rain also filleth the pools. They go from strength
to strength, every one of them in Zion appeareth before God.
—*Psalms 84:5-7*

Some Jewish scholars see the valley of Baca as a very dry place. It is a place travelers have to go through to get to the refuge cities. The valley of Baca is a place that has super deep crevices or pits and also extremely dangerous animals. *Not everyone who enters the valley of Baca makes it out.* However, the Bible encourages us that those who have their strength and hope in the Lord will indeed make it through the valley of Baca.

The word Baca means to weep. The valley of Baca is also known as the *valley of weeping* or the *valley of tears*. Baca is a place of pain and loneliness. It is a place of tears. In order to get to the "refuge" we are required to go through some times of loneliness and pain. Acts 14:22 says, "...reminding them that we must suffer many hardships to enter the Kingdom of God" (NLT). The Bible is filled with verses explaining to Christians that we *will* go through "garbage" if we intend to make Heaven our home. Baca is symbolic of the trials, ridiculously stupid circumstances, and insanely irritating suffering that we have to go through.

This "wonderful" valley of weeping is not an option of a child of God, but indeed a certainty. The valley produces maturity and character in us. This reminds me of a certain passage of scripture.

> My brethren, count it all joy when ye fall into divers temptations; Knowing this, that the trying of your faith worketh patience. But let patience have her perfect work, that ye may be perfect and entire, waiting nothing.

—James 1:2-4

I have journeyed through this valley many times, and no doubt you have too. There have been times that the only word I can use to describe it is "stupid." Pain can be stupid. Lonely days can be stupid. Sitting and crying because you are in so much pain and agony can feel stupid. But I am thankful that on those stupid days, there is Someone who counteracts all of that stupidity.

Another reason that walking through the valley of Baca is difficult is that many times one has to do it alone. Sure, we might have family or friends that are "there for us" or that are keeping us in their prayers. I don't say that flippantly; I am very thankful for those people, and I know I couldn't do life without them. But there are life lessons and there are valleys that must be conquered solo.

I remember going through something very difficult. In my alone time with God, I was bawling and begging Him to send me just one person who "gets it." All I wanted was someone to wrap me in their arms and tell me that they understood (and actually mean it). Clearly that wasn't too much to ask for? Or was it?

Apparently it was (just being real). I can't sit here and give you a list of reasons as to why we sometimes go through things alone. I can't even try to fake it and sound smart. I have nothing. . .or almost nothing. There is only one reason that I can come up with, and it seems simple. Well, in a way simple, but possibly in another way very complex. God wants us to trust Him. I could still trust God...*and* have someone right beside me. Right?

I remember reading something somewhere that said, "When Jesus is all that you have, you find that Jesus is all that you need." So maybe Jesus wants us to go through the valley solo so we can depend completely on Him. If we had others, we would depend on others. But I have found that others don't always have the answer, but Jesus always has the answer.

I have often heard that tears are a language that God understands. I have found that to be true first hand. Sadly, not everyone believes that way.

I have had multiple clients who, if they had felt complete freedom, would have busted into tears during our session. I remember asking one person why they looked so tense. They had never had someone's undivided, non-judgmental attention before. They were raised to "be seen and not heard." Wow. What a way to be raised. If you have been around for any length of time you have probably heard the cliché, "real men don't cry." Obviously, we know that is not true. Real men do cry. And that is okay. Actually, more than okay, that is good. Chuck Swindoll once said, "A teardrop on earth summons the King of heaven." Just imagine, every time a child of God cries, all of Heaven goes on alert. Even though crying can be very beneficial, I am thankful for a promise that God made that I can hold onto.

> He will wipe every tear from their eyes, and there will be no more death or sorrow or crying or pain. All these things are gone forever.
>
> —Revelation 21:4

Someone once asked me what my favorite passage in the Bible was. I quickly blurted out a scripture. . .and another. . .and another. . . and another. How can you possibly only have *one* favorite verse in the Bible? I quickly came to the conclusion that for me it is impossible to have just one. And that is totally fine. Through the last handful of years, Psalms 23 has become one of my favorite passages in the Bible. Initially, verse 4 was the one that stood out to me. After all, the words "the valley of the shadow of death" are enough to send goosebumps up and down anyone's spine. But the more I began to rely on God, the more I realized that the first verse is where the gold is at: "The Lord is my shepherd, I shall not want." I remember as a young child being confused at that verse. "I shall not want? But aren't we supposed to want God?!" With age, comes wisdom. . .or at least it should.

I have had to determine in my life the difference between wants and needs. Do I really *need* an X-large French fry, or do I just want it? Do I *need* to spend my paycheck buying new clothes, or do I just want to? Psalms 23:1 is noting the difference between a want and a need. The Lord promised to meet our needs; He didn't promise to meet our wants. Obviously, He wants us to be happy, but we also have to be realistic.

My friend walked through a valley similar to the valley of Baca or the valley of the shadow of death. She lost her father unexpectedly through an illness that should have been prevented.

This is my friend's story:

> My father went into the hospital on July 24, 2006, a whole, complete man. He had a very small, nagging cough. However, he was a whole man. On August 17, 2006 at 1:11 am, he was a dead man.
>
> Throughout my life, my dad had been sick. By the time I realized that it wasn't normal to be as familiar with the hospital and staff as I was, I was old enough to drive. The

man lived through numerous major surgeries, and it was a small surgery that finally killed him.

He finally got tired of the nagging cough that he had and went to the doctor. They diagnosed him with Pulmonary Fibroses. The only part they were uncertain of was if it was idiopathic (fatal) or stationary (curable). To find out, they needed to do a small biopsy of his lungs.

It was supposed to be a day surgery. He was to get it done and then be home that night, awaiting answers. However, he didn't come home until August 2nd. When he did come home, he was on a shockingly high amount of oxygen and was back in the hospital within a week.

The night he died I will never forget—ever. That night is burned into my brain, in a way that is far more emotional than I want to admit. He was moved to a room because he didn't need to be in ICU anymore. I'm sure he knew that he was going to die, but I wasn't quite there yet.

My mom and I left with the rest of my family around 8 pm. We got to our exit on the freeway, and she knew she needed to go back. I was fine with that; I grabbed a blanket and my phone charger and off we went, right back to Providence.

I lay on the floor in a private visiting room and was talking to a friend when my mom busted into the room and I hear her say, "Sarah, get up. Your dad is going to die tonight."

I called my family and our close friends to let them know that his time had come. I sat on a windowsill for what seemed like hours.

At one time, my brother and sister-in-law were standing on the left of my dad's bed. My mom was sitting in a chair at his right, and my pastor was standing behind her. She started sobbing, yelling, and pleading with God and my dad to let everything be okay, that she had nothing to live for without him.

I had never seen my mom break down like this before. I wasn't quite sure how to react. It was the only time that I let myself lose it in front of my mom. I knelt in front of her and cried. My breakdown caused her to focus on me, my brother, my sister-in-law. I cried until she realized that there was more than him: my dad, her husband. Was it selfish? I don't know, but I reacted before I could think of what I was doing.

After that one breakdown. I went to a numb place. My mind was blank. My thoughts were blank.

At 1:11 am, I saw my sister-in-law nod at me. My brother grabbed my pastor's hand over the bed and pulled the watch crown to stop his watch. My dad was dead. Deceased. Gone. Just a body. No spirit.

I couldn't touch him. I could hardly look at him. I cannot see his face in my head at this point. I remember his toes, uncovered at the foot of the bed, as they always were. I remember that they looked so normal, and nothing was going to be normal anymore. I let that moment sink in. His toes. His curved toenails. His pasty white feet. Nothing was going to be normal anymore. My dad was dead.

I sat in the waiting room as people talked. I talked. I was fine. I remember leaving the hospital thinking that it was finally over. The drive home, in the back of my pastor's car, was surreal. I remember calling my manager, letting her know he was dead. I remember getting home, seeing my mom to bed and talking to my pastor's wife for a few hours. Then I climbed into bed with my mom and slept, listened to her cry, and slept some more.

They say that death changes people. It's true—very true. I remember when my grandpa passed away years before.

I was broken. I couldn't stop crying. It was the first person that was close to me who died. I didn't understand it at all. I remember dinner that night. My dad was laughing and telling jokes, and I didn't understand why he wasn't feeling how I was feeling. It was his dad after all! I screamed at him for being so uncaring and ran off to my room.

After my dad died, I understood. I was the same way, laughing and telling jokes. I turned my grief into working energy. I didn't have time to cry and have a pity party. I had to figure out who was going to take care of my mom. I had to figure out how, when we were struggling to make ends meet on a two-income household, we were just going to make it on just my mom's.

I finally felt the weight of responsibility. "Take care of your mom, like your dad would" became almost a mantra to me. I am sure I failed miserably, but it was the only thing I knew to do.

I think that the hardest part of this whole thing was trying to grieve like others wanted me to grieve. I got some comments from my mom at one point, telling me that she didn't think I had grieved. Just because I didn't grieve in the way that everyone else did, doesn't mean I didn't let myself grieve in the way that was healthy for me.

The only time I remember letting myself grieve in a way that would seem normal to others was when I was praying. During those times, I was able to let myself pour out my heart to God. I didn't feel bad laying my burdens on Him. He was my safe place.

Getting used to a new normal was different. It took years to figure out how to cook for two and not four. Holidays were the worst. In the earliest years, the gaping hole was obvious. We hardly celebrated because the hole was that large.

The hours turned into days, the days turned to weeks, weeks to months, and months to years. Ten years later, that girl of twenty-three is now thirty-three.

I still feel a weight of responsibility. I have an aging mother that I have to take care of still. If I don't, there is no one else. As I get older, the ache of not having my dad around is even clearer. My brother has had four children who never met their grandfather. If I ever get married, my dad won't walk me down the aisle. If I have children, they will never know my dad. Some of my closest friends do not know my father.

Holidays have gotten a lot easier. We even decorate now. Father's Day is still hands down the worst day. It never gets easier.

Because I am a lot like my father, jokes helped me over any of the hard times. Still to this day, I am joking about it. I feel like, if my dad were alive, he would be laughing right alongside me.

I remember going over to their house just hours after my friend's father died. I went over with another friend to make dinner for them. I had no idea what to expect. I will admit, I was thrown off guard for a bit. My friend and her brother were sitting in the dining room… laughing. Laughing? I didn't know what to do with this. I asked the person who I went with, "Why are they cracking jokes and laughing? Don't they know their dad just died?" I thought crying was the only way to cope with such a tragedy. I settled in and was eventually comfortable with the laughter. Her mother came out to the family room from her bedroom. Now I really didn't know what to do. She sat on the couch and would just start crying. Her tears would subside and it appeared as though things were under control. It would be just a few minutes later that the tears would start again.

I was pretty young during that time. I didn't understand the grieving process. I didn't understand loss to that magnitude. But you know what? I didn't have to. It wasn't my place to come up with the correct things to say. It was my job to just be there. There are times when silence literally is golden.

Crying is okay. In fact, crying is cathartic and healing. Just as though someone puts antibiotic cream on a cut for it to heal, so our body produces tears to heal our soul.

I am glad that there is a God who can see us in our hurt, frustration, or pain. Instead of turning our face from Him, we need to find our strength *in* Him. If we turn from the valley of Baca, we will miss out on our promise that is on the other side. I am thankful that even though we have to go through the *valley of tears*, God promises that He will meet us there.

CHAPTER 4

IT'S THE CLIMB

*Success is not final, failure is not final: it is
the courage to continue that counts.*
—*Winston Churchill*

t has always been my dream to climb Mt. Everest. Well, *my*
Mt. Everest has a different name—other people like to call it
Multnomah Falls. As a child and teenager, I could only make it up
to the first bridge. Climbing up a mountain with my level of asthma
generally doesn't make for a positive outcome. But of course I didn't
let that stop me...from trying at least.

I am smart enough to know that it would *not* be smart for me
to try doing it solo. I planned on finding someone as crazy as I was
(or even more so). After some coercion, two of my friends and I
decided to go and climb Multnomah Falls. The prep work was pretty
humorous. I filled my backpack with quite the exhaustive list: eight
frozen water bottles, Kleenex, allergy pills, inhalers, deodorant, gum,
medical tape, lotion, and mints. I had never taken a "Surviving the
Wilderness" class before, but I knew that I had to go prepared (lotion
is going to get me real far in life). I had basically planned on us getting
lost in the mountainous terrain and stranded on the south side of the
Columbia Gorge. There were many scenarios that I allowed to play

through my mind, one of which was that we were going to be stuck up there for two weeks until someone found us huddling together and sharing pieces of gum. If by chance we died, the rescuers would have no doubt found little messages in the dirt from us to our loved ones.

The day was finally here! We were to meet at 10 in the morning. It was my day off, and waking up that early was a miracle, so they definitely knew I was serious about this life-risking hike. I got my things and started walking to my car. To get to my car, I have to walk up this *very* slight incline. By the time I got to the top of the "hill," I was already huffing and puffing. I thought to myself, "What on earth are you doing, Amber?!"

When we all met, one of my friends suggested that we climb an easier path and slowly prepare our bodies to climb my Mt. Everest. I shot that idea down *very* quickly. It was all or nothing for me. If I am going to risk my life, then I am going to risk it on something *big!*

Most of the population I currently work with are those that have substance abuse problems. They admit that they want to quit, but one year sober seems *impossible!* So I like to draw out a diagram for my clients. I draw a picture of a mountain. I put an X at the base of the mountain, which represents where they are, and I put an X at the top of the mountain, which is what they want their end goal to be. When my clients look all the way to the top of the mountain is seems like such a daunting task to maintain sobriety and stay out of trouble with the law for one year. But then I start breaking up the mountain into many little goals. I encourage them to set many little goals instead of focusing on the *giant* impossible goal. Instead of one year sober, why not make it one week? At the end of the week, we can acknowledge the accomplishment. Before they know it, a month has passed, six months, ten months, and then one year!

When people decide that they want to climb the real Mt. Everest, they don't just wake up one morning and decide they will climb it the next day. It takes a very disciplined, rigorous training schedule. Once they start at the base of the mountain, they don't just plan on going straight up with no breaks. Their goal is to make it to the first camp, and then the next, and so on. They set their eyes on the landmarks.

I can't remember how, but my friend somehow changed my mind and so we decided to start on a smaller path that wasn't as steep. This was still fine because it was going to be a great day and *any* type of accomplishment would be good for me.

We found a general area to start walking. We started this hike and we heard a waterfall. There was a fork in the road, and we decided to follow the waterfall. It sounded super close. We thought all we had to do was walk a little bit up the path and we would find it. We were mistaken. The woods seemed to be playing tricks on us. We finally decided to turn and go back. When we came to the original fork, I got this bright idea of following that path to see where it would take us. One of my friends was too tired, but the other one agreed to go with me. And so we went.

I apologized several times to her because we walked about 15 feet and had to take a break. We repeated this pattern continuously until we finished. About halfway through, I stopped and told her that I couldn't go on. She encouraged me to not quit and to keep going. And so I did...probably against *all* medical advice.

We were walking uphill the whole time. We arrived to this leveled-out landing area where we could look out and see the Columbia River Gorge and see how high we were. It already felt as though we were on top of the world! The view was breathtaking (pun intended). I did not realize how far we had come. We saw a family that was walking toward us from the direction that we were going. I asked the lady how far the waterfall was. Her daughter anxiously told us that it was "right around the corner" and to "not give up." We smiled real big and got a second wind. We were bound and determined to get to the waterfall.

"Right around the corner" ended up not being right around the corner, but I just couldn't give up. I had made up in my mind to finish what I had started. The only way I was going to stop was if I had to be carried off by a medical team. We finally made it to the waterfall. We sat for about 20 minutes and talked about the beauty that God created. I felt...accomplished. We took several pictures and decided to head back because our other friend was waiting in the car for our safe return.

As we were making our way back to the car, we started talking about parallels in this journey that we call life. For some, it can be easy to walk out on God when things get hard. It sounds appealing to go sit in the car with air conditioning instead of climbing two miles uphill. We quit when life gets hard. However, that only results in short-term benefits. If I would have given up, then I would not have the long-term benefits such as looking back years later and still being proud of myself that I finished.

My grandmother has said many times, "Amber, anything in life worth having is worth working for." Was it hard for me to climb two miles? For sure. I was tired, in pain, and hungry. But I can still say now that I am *so* thankful that I continued on and didn't quit. Even if it did nothing for my body, it did something for my spirit. It taught me a valuable life lesson. For some people, a two-mile hike could seem like nothing. To me, it seemed just short of climbing Mt. Everest. When life hurts, we keep on going.

The next day, a group of my youth group and I actually went to Multnomah Falls. Here was my chance! I got my backpack with a bunch of water bottles and I was ready yet again. I didn't even wait for everyone. I got out of the car and started my hike of a lifetime. I got to the first bridge and was still alive! I just knew that in about another hour I would be standing on top of the world.

I got about 1/5 of the way between the first bridge and the second bridge and had to stop. The rest of my group quickly passed me, and I was now in the very back. I stood there bending over, deciding if I could go on or not. As I was debating in my mind, I noticed a little girl that was skipping from the top of the falls to the bottom. She came up to me and stopped. She had an irritatingly big smile on her face. I say irritating because *no one* should have a smile on after climbing the whole thing and being on their way back down. But this girl was different. She looked eye level with me (since I was bending over) and said, "Don't give up! It's worth the view! Whatever you do, don't give up!" I had this deadpan look on my face. Part of me was irritated at her for being so happy and part of me was in shock.

Oh, how that statement fits into our lives! Whenever I have been in the middle of something hard, that little girl pops into my head. I have to tell myself, "Amber, it will be worth it! Whatever you do, don't give up." Because of that statement, I have accomplished many more things in life. "Amber, stay in school. It will be worth it when you finally have your Master's degree." "Amber, keep working on your music projects! You will be glad that you didn't quit when it is finished." Of course the best one, "Amber, don't give up on God! You will be glad when you get to Heaven!" I am reminded of a favorite verse that is near and dear to my heart.

> But they that wait upon the LORD shall renew *their* strength; they shall mount up with wings as eagles; they shall run, and not be weary; *and* they shall walk, and not faint.
>
> —Isaiah 40:31

When going through crisis or trauma, the last thing we want to do is keep fighting. It would be much easier just to stay in bed with the lights off and not get up. But we have to keep going. However, that does not mean that we shouldn't allow time for the grieving process. Everyone is different and everyone needs to grieve on their own timeline.

This was a lighter story. Not all stories have good endings like this one. Not all stories are full of inspiration and encouragement.

There are times when we work so hard just to find one ray of hope, and if we look through our human eye, we might not even see any. This is one of the many reasons why it is imperative to have a personal relationship with Jesus. When we look around and can't find anything worth living for, we can look to God, who in turn will show us many reasons to live.

> Looking unto Jesus the author and finisher of our faith; who for the joy that was set before him endured the cross, despising the shame, and is set down at the right hand of the throne of God.
>
> —Hebrews 12:2

He is the One that gives us the reason to live. He is the author of our lives. He knows the end from the beginning. He knows all of the good days, as well as the bad days. He also knows our hurts. And I am thankful that He understands us and is with us when life hurts.

Chapter 5

DEATH CEASES TO CARE

Hardships often prepare ordinary people for an extraordinary destiny.
—*C.S. Lewis*

Death is something that some people find awkward to talk about. It can be uncomfortable. But why? We want to go to Heaven so bad and we talk about longing for that day...but we fear death. Why is that? If you're hoping I will give an answer, you will be hoping for a very long time. I don't have an answer. Maybe for the fear of the unknown? Maybe because we know that we won't ever see our loved ones on earth again? Or possibly we might not do very well with goodbyes and death appears like a permanent goodbye? Or perhaps we are unsure if we are ready to meet the Lord? There could be many reasons.

I worked at a job where I delivered medication to hospice patients. Some of them lived in nursing homes and care centers, but most of them lived in their own houses. I worked that job for just over a year. In that year I saw some scenarios that were, for lack of a better word, beautiful. The family and close friends were all there. The patient had taken care of everything and was in good spirits. Closure had been made. It was just a matter of time.

Death can be beautiful, but it can also be...gnarly. One of the patients that I delivered to was an older gentleman. At this point he was still able to work and walk around....and smoke and drink. There had been a communication problem between the pharmacy, my company, and the doctor's office. The patient didn't get his medication on time, and I had to make the delivery a day late. I was hoping it would be an easy, quick delivery—wishful thinking.

I went to the front door and his caregiver answered the door and signed for the medication. So far so good. Now all I had to do was make it back to my car. I noticed the garage door was opened and I tried to hide behind the cars so the person in the garage didn't see me. No such luck. The patient was in the garage, smoking and working on a project. He saw my blue polo and got my attention by screaming and yelling. He asked why he didn't get his meds. I politely apologized for my company the best that I knew how.

He continued to yell. For a split second I started to get irritated, but I quickly remembered an important detail about this patient. He was dying. So I gave him the benefit of the doubt. I told him to yell at me all he wanted. I stood there still and let him put a sailor to shame. At the end of his venting, he asked, "Do you know what it's like to not be able to breathe?!" His voice inflections made it a rhetorical question or perhaps implied that I had *no* idea what that was like.

He waited for an answer. I looked him straight in the eyes and said with a calm voice, "Yes, sir. I do." He looked very stunned. I think I threw him off guard. He probably wasn't prepared for that response. He quickly apologized for getting mad at me when technically it was out of my control. I talked with him for a few more minutes until he calmed down and then went back to work. I got in my car, drove away, and as soon as I was out of sight I parked my car and just sat in the quietness of the evening. What in the world had just happened?! I was able to get a little glimpse into the hearts of people who are dying.

Death does not discriminate. Death does not care if you are

two days old or 200 years old. Death does not care if you have led a seemingly perfect life or if your life is the definition of dysfunctional. Death does not care if you have been healthy your whole entire life or if you have been sick more days than not. Death just does not care.

There was another man that I will never forget. I had instructions to go to the back door when I arrived. I knocked on the door and didn't hear anything. I looked inside and I couldn't see anyone. I tried one more time. Finally, I heard a quiet voice beckoning for me to come in. I followed the voice, and it was the patient lying in bed. He had lost both of his legs and had a huge whole in his abdomen area. He was on oxygen and had many pill bottles next to his bed. Just out of habit, I asked how he was doing.

I remember thinking how stupid I was for asking such a question. Of course he was not good! How could he be?! Since I asked such a question, I prepared myself for a very long detailed answer. I thought he was going to talk about how much pain he was in and how he was not ready to die. His answer threw me off guard. With a soft smile on his face, he humbly answered "I'm doing pretty good. And yourself?" *What? You're doing good!? You don't have legs! You're dying! You have a hole the size of a tennis ball on your stomach! How can you be good?! And why in the world are you asking about me?! Who cares about ME! You're the one dying!* Those were the thoughts that were going through my mind. Of course, I answered with the normal, "Oh, I am great! Thank you for asking." I couldn't be completely honest with him. I was a stranger to him. Clearly he didn't really want me to actually answer. Did he? Could it have been possible that he actually wanted me to answer how I was really doing? To him, it could have been a momentary diversion from the obvious (death). But to me, I couldn't allow myself to vent about frivolous things such as what I was dealing with. Could it have been possible that with not being honest to him I made the moment about me? I don't know. I'm just throwing the idea out there.

When I started my internship at the Washington County Jail

in Hillsboro, OR, there was another intern doing the same type of work. She was from George Fox University. At that time, she was about halfway through her work at the jail. I tried to look like I knew exactly what I was doing, but let's be real…I really had *no* idea what was going on. If we were to count the questions, I probably asked her at least a quarter of a million questions…in the first week. We spent a lot of time "consulting" each other about current cases.

People that go into counseling generally have dealt with crises many times in their lives. They understand the importance of a nonjudgmental listening ear and therefore they want to provide the same type of support to others in need.

My friend definitely has had her share of ups and downs. She lost her father when she was in graduate school. There never is a right time for tragedy to strike, but it always seems like the moment you least expect something to happen, it happens.

This is my friend's story:

> Grad school is stressful. It was very stressful for my new friends who were following up their undergraduate degrees with a Master's degree. It was another type of stress for my friends who were young mothers trying to juggle family life and studies, and for me, at 55, I experienced another brand of stress. I started my undergraduate studies along with my youngest children—they were 18 and I was in my late 40s. It was a dream come true for me to finally be pursuing my education, and I knew full well with the major I chose that it would be about an eight-year journey.
>
> At the beginning of my 3rd year of graduate school, I experienced a chain of events that made being in school a much greater challenge than I ever expected. I loved learning and I was a good student, but this moment in time stretched me farther than I would have ever dreamed possible.

The fall term had just begun and I was ready to dig in. By this time, I had a pretty workable routine. I worked three days a week at a medical clinic, went to school two nights a week, and spent the weekends writing papers in the comfort of my cozy home. First, we had a fire break out on our back deck, causing quite a bit of damage and requiring us to be relocated to a hotel in downtown Portland—one that would accommodate my little family of three and our two dogs. We took about a week's worth of clothes with us and the personal items we thought we would need but soon found out it would be three months before we could go home. All of our possessions were out of our reach, being treated for smoke damage, so that was frustrating to say the least—inconvenient but doable. I did my homework on a hotel bed while my husband and son watched TV nearby.

During this time, I really began to worry about my dad. I called and left messages for my stepmother three times within the four days leading up to his passing but didn't get a response. Finally, while sitting in class, I got a text message from her asking me to call her. Even though it wasn't appropriate to do so in class, I texted back asking her if something was wrong, and she simply said yes. She asked if I could call at 8 pm because there were people there attending to my dad and she would have time to talk to me when they left. I got out of class at 7 pm, drove back to the hotel, and waited impatiently for 8 pm to come so I could call back—all the while, knowing he wasn't doing well and trying to figure out how I could get away from work and school long enough to get down to California to tell my dad goodbye. When I did call, she answered the phone crying, telling me that my dad had just died. I was too late; I didn't get to say goodbye.

It was too much. My home was in shambles; I was hanging

on by a thread trying to deal with the insurance company and the restoration company and surviving in a hotel, all while trying to keep up with my job and my schoolwork. Now I'd lost my first true love. I wanted to give up; I felt abandoned by my dad and also by God. The wave of grief felt like it would drown me. How could I continue to hold it all together when I just wanted to curl up in a ball and cry?

Like most, I was a daddy's girl. He was an educator, and my fondest memories are of the summers when he would take me to school and allow me to work with him. I wanted to be just like him and teach when I grew up. He was my hero. When my parents divorced and my dad got remarried, my stepmother had a hard time accepting me, and it always left me longing for the kind of relationship I once had with him. As he aged, I worried about bitterness and how I would possibly go to his funeral one day and try to comfort his wife when she had made it so difficult for me to enjoy my dad over most of my life, but God has a way of changing hearts.

My dad was 92 when he passed away, but when he was approaching 88, my stepmother called and asked me if they could come up and celebrate his birthday with us in Portland. Of course, I was thrilled. He was already suffering from dementia by then, but he still knew me and we had a very sweet visit that I treasure in my heart to this day. From that time on, she worked at developing a relationship with me, and by the time my father passed away, the bitterness was gone and we were able to share a loss that was overwhelming for both of us. He was my daddy and he was her husband. We both loved him and we both had broken hearts. I didn't foresee it ending that way, as I ached for my dad over many years, wondering why she didn't want me involved in their lives.

I have to give God all the credit for seeing me through that season, starting with the fire, followed by the loss of my Dad—all the while helping me maintain the grades I needed to complete that semester of graduate school. The funeral I'd dreaded all my adult life never happened; she just couldn't face her friends and loved ones gathering to say goodbye while she felt so broken. I understood, and I was able to grieve at home, with my husband and children around me, still attending classes and going to work like I needed to do. It was a hard and sad time, but by the sweet grace of God, I was able to get through it and forge an emotional bond with my stepmother even though I never believed it was possible.

Fast forwarding a year and a half, I graduated with my Master's degree in counseling; I had secured employment as a counselor along with a supplemental position as an adjunct professor at the university I'd attended for the past eight years.

A graduation gift arrived in the mail from my stepmother: a golden apple that was given to my father when he retired from his position as the principal of an elementary school after 26 years. It has a place of pride in my new therapy office now, and I thank God every time I see it for the wonderful father he gave me, the ability to follow in his footsteps as an educator, and, finally, for the restoration of a very strained relationship with my stepmom.

I can't even begin to imagine what this was like...for all of this to happen right in the middle of graduate school. But I can imagine that the pain seemed unbearable to manage at times. Even in the midst of tragedy, God has a way of letting the sun shine...in some way or another. Out of a heavy rain comes freshly watered roses. Do you ever "get over" something like this? I don't think so. Honestly, that term irritates me. "Get over it" is a past-tense term. Why are we in such a hurry to rush the healing process? Healing from crisis and trauma takes time. It may even take years. Sometimes it might even take the rest of your life. And that is okay.

Can you even move on from such a tragic loss? To me, when I hear "move on," I think of leaving something behind. I don't think this is normal either, because when you lose someone, you carry their memories wherever you go. However, I think it is possible for one to work through a loss. Working through something doesn't mean you get over it or you move on life. It means that you are able to process the reality that loss took place and still do life.

Chapter 6

HE'LL MAKE A WAY. CLEARLY

When one door of happiness close, another opens; but
often we look so long at the closed door that we do
not see the one which has been opened for us.
—*Helen Keller.*

Crisis and trauma for one person might be completely different for the next. Each person experiences pain that is unique to their own self. Just like the grieving process, everyone's threshold for crisis is different. When comparing losses, some losses may appear greater than another loss to humans because we tend to compare them on a scale between no crisis and the worst possible situation ever. But fact of the matter is that all loss hurts in some way or another. All losses are painful. I continue to shock myself. I can be very calm when it comes to crazy intense situations that involve other people, but at the same time I can have a complete meltdown at something that might seem like no big deal to the next person. It's amazing how God made us all different.

Something like that happened to me on February 27, 2011. That is a day that I can *almost* guarantee that I will never forget, mainly because of the traumatic situation, but also because that is when my niece was born.

Approximately a month prior to this specific day, I was given a very nice Pearl drum kit from my stepdad. He had spent years adding pieces and making it *very* nice. It was my baby. I was planning on keeping it in the family for the next 60 years. I would give it to my kids and they would give it to their kids. But life doesn't always go the way that we plan.

I had set up the kit at a local church, as they did not have a set. On Saturday night (the night prior to the event), I brought the kit home to clean and polish it. I spent several hours cleaning every inch of the kit. It was beautiful. I was a proud new momma. I had my first drum kit. My niece was on her way. Life was great.

I don't know what I was thinking, but I loaded my kit up in my car that night and was planning on taking it to church Sunday. Sunday morning came. I woke up and felt like a new woman! I was headed out to my car with my very large purse and Bible in one hand and two cymbal stands in the other. I walked up the small incline and turned the corner. My life came to a halting stop. There was nothing in my car.

I slowly walked to my car, opened the door, and threw my purse in the back, along with the cymbal stands. My first reaction was, "I'm going to kill my friends! This is a *horrible* joke." How could this have happened? Why did this happen? I knew if I freaked out physically that I would have to just go straight to the ER instead of church. Physiologically, I was calm. Psychologically, I was a wreck.

I got in the driver's seat and just sat there. I immediately texted a few of my close friends just in case they had pulled a *sick* joke on me. I definitely wouldn't put it past them. They all denied doing anything. I was hoping it was them, but it wasn't. I didn't know what to do.

I turned on my car and the song on the CD that was automatically playing was "When God Unfolds the Rose" (He always gets it right). I thought that was ironic but clearly was not in the mood for such jokes. I held back the tears as long as I could. Before I knew it, the flood gates had opened. There was no holding back. It took me about twelve minutes to drive to church, and the whole time I was driving I was crying. I sat in the car for a few minutes trying to compose myself. I finally was ready to go inside...or so I thought.

The first thing I did was go and talk to the other drummer. I was on the schedule to play during the night service and not the morning. I asked him if I could play both services because I needed to be in my comfort zone. I need to be somewhere familiar. I started to uncontrollably cry and had to just stop talking. He said that he had no problem with me playing both services.

Before Sunday School started, I went and sat on the second pew from the front. I just sat and stared at the ground. I couldn't even pray. It wasn't because I was so mad at God, but I just couldn't talk or I would start crying again. I called my mother and told her what had happened. How on earth was I supposed to tell my stepdad? I just couldn't, so she had agreed to break the news to him.

I didn't even bother to go to Sunday School. I didn't want people to ask questions. I was in no mood to sit with a fake smile on my face and tell my story so casually. Not only was I not in the mood, but I couldn't possibly make myself do it.

I played the drums during song service. Up to that point, the drums were the only thing keeping me somewhat sane. I remember tears streaming down my face the whole time. At that point, I was fine with people seeing me cry because they were probably thinking that I was just getting blessed by the Lord. That was far from the truth. I was bawling because I was so mad. Mad at God? No. I was mad at the people who seemed heartless that broke into my car and took my drums. I was mad at myself for thinking that the drums would be okay in my car overnight. There was no way to sugarcoat it. I was just mad.

It was offering time. Something very unexpected happened. My pastor got up and told the church what had just taken place. He announced that the cash offering that came in would go to me to buy another kit. The tears started flowing once again. Something else that was in my car that got stolen was my breathing machine for asthma. What sick and twisted person would do that?! There was about $2,000 worth of equipment stolen out of my car. I was not expecting my pastor to do that at all, and that was a big blessing.

I think God knew what I was feeling. It is amazing how He could see me specifically out of all the people in this world. I received a phone call at about two o'clock that afternoon from my very pregnant sister. She casually told me she had just got to the hospital and was in labor! The second that I heard that, my day had completely made a turnaround. I completely forgot about the turmoil that I was in. I rushed to the hospital thinking that the baby was coming *now!* I clearly did not know what the actual definition of "labor" meant. Hours later, my niece graced this world with her presence. The day that started out horribly ended wonderfully.

Even now, when I think about that drum kit, I get a feeling on anger and have to force myself to think about something else. Some people may read this and think, "I thought this book was about life hurting, and instead I am reading about such silliness." For me, that day hurt. It will always hurt. It is not about the details specifically, but it is about how it hurt. That was something near and dear to my heart. That was a great loss that I had to face. Think about a loss in your life that was important to you. Remember how bad it hurt? Did you wonder why other people weren't feeling the same kind of pain? That is because your heart was invested in a way that nobody else understood. Or so you thought. There is One who will always understand.

Chapter 7

LONELY, BUT NEVER ALONE

*If you had never known physical pain in your life,
how could you appreciate the nail scarred hands
with which Jesus Christ will meet you?*
—Joni Eareckson Tada

About four years ago, I went through a very painful season—a season where I felt very lonely. You know the kind that I am talking about—the kind when you can be in a room full of people but feel like you are the only one there. Those times are hard. That is when you learn to rely wholeheartedly on God to keep you company.

Every summer, youth groups that I am associated with meet at a campground for four days. Youth camp was always the highlight of my year. For years, we went to Camp Arrah Wanna in Welches, OR. I had gone to youth camp as a camper one last time. I knew that I was getting too old and that the next year I would "upgrade" to a camp counselor. It was during the worst season of the year—allergy season. It looked like it was snowing because of all the pollen and cottonwood flying around. This one particular year, five minutes after we arrived on campus, I started to wheeze. I knew right away that this was going to be a rough camp.

Every year I went there I would have bad asthma problems. But did that stop me from going the next year? Of course not! Anyway, I didn't tell anyone that I was already having problems because I did not want to be sent home. What kid wants to be sent home from youth camp? Not me!

There was a Respiratory Therapist (RT) that was attending as a counselor. Monday night I went and introduced myself to her. I was curious about RT work because that was something I was interested in and something that was near and dear to my heart (or to my lungs). We sat and talked for a while, and I honestly didn't expect to develop any kind of relationship with her. That changed—very quickly.

That night was a very rough night for me. I still didn't want to tell anyone, but it was hard to hide a very loud thick wheeze. Somehow, someone got the RT to come and look at me. She and the camp nurse decided to take me into Portland to go to the urgent care to get some steroids. Oh joy. Prednisone. Just what everyone wants.

The clinic we went to was...ridiculous. I knew what needed to happen. The RT knew what needed to happen. Apparently the doctor missed the memo. He listened to my lungs and noted that there was some fluid in them. Of course there was! We already knew that. We were wanting him to tell us something we didn't know. My five-year-old niece knows more than that doctor did. He gave me a prescription for an inhaler, and off we went back to camp. Something that is common knowledge is you should try and stay *away* from triggers... not run back to them. However, it was youth camp. Of course I was going to go back.

I slept the rest of the day on Tuesday. I slept all day Wednesday. I slept most of Thursday. All I was doing was sleeping...and apparently dying.

Thursday night came. We were having our last church service. Everyone else was standing during song service, and I was sitting there trying to breathe. I thought I was doing a great job hiding the sickness, but apparently I forgot there was an RT there whose job it was to notice signs that most people don't. I felt someone put their hand on my back, and I opened my eyes and turned. It was the head counselor. She had a sympathetic smile on her face and I knew what that meant. Ugh. I was having to go home.

I picked up my Bible and my purse and went outside. There were four other adults trying to figure out what to do. We called my father, and he said it was my choice and that I was an adult. Of course, I wanted to stay until it was over. After a long conversation, we all decided that I would stay through the volleyball all-star game and then head home that night. I was fine with those results.

Church service was over but there were still a few more people praying. By this time, I was exhausted. I literally had no more strength to stay awake or keep my head up. I quietly sat in a chair and leaned up against the wall. The RT came over to me and asked how I was doing. I remember saying something along the lines of, "I'm tired of breathing." I had spent four days of hard labored breathing and it was exhausting.

That is the last thing I remember. Apparently, after a while they were trying to decide if they should call 911 or not. They finally did. Per the RT, my chest wasn't rising, my heart wasn't beating, and my fingers were turning blue. They also said that I was extremely pale and looked dead. I have no idea how long I was out for.

The next thing I remember was a female firefighter reaching up my dress to put the heart monitor things on my chest. Before I knew it they were placing me on a stretcher and loading me into the ambulance. The RT road with me because I needed someone to advocate for me, and I clearly was in no position of doing that alone.

Shockingly, I was doing good enough that the ER let me go home around 1 a.m. I went and filled my prescription for prednisone and then went home and crashed. You know that cliché, "I'm dying from exhaustion!" Yeah. That was real. That was me. I was dying from exhaustion that week.

I have no idea what it was, but something happened in my body that night. I no longer could get warm. I was cold *all* of the time. I would sit in 102-degree weather with a hoody on and cuddled up in a blanket. Thankfully, within the last year, my body has gone back to normal.

I had to take work completely off for two weeks. At that time, I was working as a personal trainer at the local gym. It took me about a month to get my strength completely back. That was hard. Yes, God breathed life back into my life (which I am very thankful for), but trying to understand everything from a human perspective was next to impossible. Why did God let that happen? Surely, He could have prevented any of that from happening, but He didn't.

Someone recently asked me, "Amber, after having asthma all of these years and almost dying who knows how many times, what has asthma taught you?" Wow. That's a loaded question. I sat there quietly for about 25 seconds. I wasn't thinking about what it has taught me; I was just trying to think how I could word it in a way where I wouldn't cry. "It has taught me to be strong, and to trust God."

If you're an asthmatic, then chances are you're a fighter. You can't have such a chronic disease and not be a fighter. Those of you who have CF, COPD, lung cancer/disease will understand. Every day is a fight. It would be easy to just give up. But we can't, so we fight.

There have been many days where I literally have had to think about my every breath. And there was the possibility of my next breath not coming (as is with everyone). To *say* you trust God is one thing, but to *believe* that you trust God is something completely different.

CHAPTER 8

HURRY UP AND WAIT!

*When a train goes through a tunnel and it gets dark, you don't throw
away the ticket and jump off. You sit still and trust the engineer.*
—Corrie Ten Boom

The next three weeks were like a whirlwind. I remember it like
yesterday, but at the same time, a lot of it still seems like a fog.
Before I went to youth camp, I noticed something growing
on my thigh. I went to camp, and as soon as I started having asthma
complications I completely forgot about the growth. About a week
after camp, I remembered it and looked to see if it was gone. Much
to my dismay, it was still there. I called my doctor's office and they
asked if I could come in that day. Sure. I asked what time and they
said, "What about in 15 minutes?" Goodness. Is it that serious? I
agreed to go in.

My normal doctor was busy, and so I had one of the other doctors
look at me. He took one look at the growth and said that we needed to
get it removed—that day. They gave me a shot of local anesthetic and
cut it off. I left the office, and by the next morning I had forgotten
about it. I didn't think anything would come of it.

One week went by…and then another.

It was a Friday morning. I had received a call from the doctor but I just let it go to voicemail. I listened to it and he had asked me to call right away. I was still in the process of waking up but decided to call him nonetheless. He said, "The pathology report came back." Pathology? What was he talking about? When did I have something go to pathology? And then I remembered what had happened two weeks prior.

The next words that came from his mouth changed the course of my life. It's amazing how much can change in just a matter of seconds. "It appears as though you have low-grade lymphoma." Lymphoma? As in cancer? It couldn't be. Is there another disease that is called lymphoma? I couldn't have cancer. That is something that happens to other people...but me? Goodness, no. I was in school full time *and* I already had asthma. I can't have *two* potentially fatal diseases at the same time. Clearly there was a mix-up in the reports...or so I wanted to believe.

Unfortunately, cancer doesn't discriminate. Cancer didn't look at my life circumstances to determine if it would plague my body or not. Cancer doesn't wait until you are out of school. Cancer doesn't wait until your children are grown and out of the house. Cancer doesn't wait for that moment when you are ROCK solid with your faith in God. Cancer just doesn't wait.

The doctor referred me to apparently one of the best oncologists in the Portland area. Generally, when faced with that type of crisis, I know I have to fight. I know I have to advocate for my own self. I didn't freak out or shut down. As soon as I hung up the phone, I called the oncology office. They were waiting for my file to be faxed from my doctor's office. So I had to wait. Sounds kind of ironic. Hurry up and wait! I have to hurry up to get into the doctors and now they tell me I have to wait. And so began the seemingly daunting task of waiting.

I walked out of my room, and just has my dad was about to leave, I told him the doctor called me back. He stopped and waited to hear what I had to say. Very casually and possibly flippantly, I said, "The pathology report came back and it was lymphoma. Apparently I have cancer." It was easy for me to say it very cognitively because it had not sunk in that I had cancer. It seemed just like another random useless fact.

The next day, the oncology clinic called to schedule an appointment. Generally, it would have taken weeks for me to get in, but she asked if I could come the next morning. I quickly agreed, as I wanted some answers. We set the appointment for 7 am the next morning. I was wide awake at 5 am...clearly something was wrong! The clinic wasn't even "officially" open yet. All that was in the office was the one oncologist and a medical assistant. I took my father with me, thinking that I wouldn't remember anything since I am supposed to not be handling it well. I think I handled it better than he did. After all, it was my life we were talking about and not my child's life. If it would have been my child's life, then I am sure I would have officially freaked out. I know what I can handle when I am sick, but if someone else is very sick I go crazy! I don't know what they are feeling. I don't know what they are experiencing. And that is hard for me to deal with.

We signed in and were ushered to the oncologist's office. I walked in and the first word I said was, "Wow!" The whole feel of the office was incredible. It had a very warm feeling to it, and there were bookshelves and, not only that, but bookshelves full of...books! Not cute little decorations, but actual books. I was in awe. After I made myself at home, I sat down on a nice plush couch. It was silent for a few minutes. I started to realize where I was. I was in the office of one of the best oncologists in the Portland metro area—not for anyone else, but for me.

As soon as the realization came over me, the oncologist walked in the office. I thrive in moments of crisis (with others), and when my flight or fight response is activated, I fight. I treated this time like one of those moments. I couldn't allow myself to have a meltdown. That was not an option. I knew I had to be my own advocate. I had to find out the details. I had to pay attention to the prognosis and diagnosis.

The oncologist had printed off my whole entire medical history through the health system company that I had been a part of for many years. She brought up things that I totally forgot ever happened. She educated us on what lymphoma is, even though I clearly already knew everything, seeing as I had spent the previous five days on Google. But I listened respectfully anyway.

She had no answers as far as a diagnosis at that point. The original pathologist sent my sample to multiple pathologists and they all agreed on the same results, that it was...weird. Of course. I wasn't shocked about that in the least bit. The first plan of action was to get a PET scan. When I had my seizure I had to have a CAT scan, so I was at least familiar with a small portion of the process (even though they are different). We said our goodbyes and scheduled the PET scan.

It was one thing to hear that I have cancer, but to actually start the staging process and possible treatment?! Surely this wasn't happening. But apparently it was. We had scheduled the PET scan for nine days away, on Friday morning at 7 am. I don't know why these medical people like getting started so early, but I figured the earlier it was the sooner I would get results. However, I quickly found out that is not how it works.

On Monday, after my initial consultation, I received something in the mail. This is when things started getting real. I got a flyer from the east coast that was about cancer support. I also got something from my university (Liberty University Online) that was about living with cancer for young adults. What in the world?! There is *no* way that Liberty could have found out that fast. I was kind of creeped out by that. Those two items were the firsts of many that I would receive in the mail about cancer.

Before I knew it, it was Friday morning. Was this really happening? Yes. Yes, it was. I met my youth pastor's wife at the hospital entrance at 7 in the morning. Originally, I thought I could do it by myself. But the more I thought about it, the more I realized that it might be good to have someone else with me. I had no idea the type of emotions that I would be experiencing. After all, I had never done this before. It was a first for me.

I asked the lady at the front desk where I should go to have a PET scan and she instructed for us to go down to the basement and there would be signs leading to Nuclear Medicine. Nuclear Medicine? Immediately my heart started beating faster than normal. But I didn't show my fear to anyone. People do this all of the time. Surely I could too. But could I? I'd like to think that I could plow through it with no problems...but I honestly had no idea what would happen. Would I freak out? Would I break down in uncontrollable sobs? Would I just deal with it and outwardly look calm, cool, and collected?

We exited the elevator in the basement. It was carpeted and nice, but it was still eerie. The temperature in the hallway was perfect, but it still sent chills up and down my spine. We walked down the hall and saw the sign—Nuclear Medicine. I stood outside of the door for just a second. Was I ready for this? No. No, I wasn't, but I had no choice. We walked in and were the only ones in the waiting room, which was nice. I was not really wanting to see other cancer patients with their bodies shutting down. I wasn't prepared to see what cancer could do to someone.

The lady at the front desk was a cancer patient herself. Her hair was just starting to grow back. She was super helpful and very kind. I acted tough, but I surely didn't feel tough. I signed in and the lady gave me a cup full to the brim of this absolutely horrible stuff you have to drink. I can still taste it, yet I can't describe how it tastes. Some say that there isn't a flavor, but there definitely is a taste. It is thick and grainy. Perhaps like white chalk? She instructed me to drink as much of it as I could before making my way back to the preparation room.

This was the time I was thankful that someone had come with me. My "support group" was able to talk to me while I was drinking that nasty stuff. If you have had a PET scan then you know exactly what I am talking about, and I am sure that you are probably reliving your experience with it as well right now (sorry!).

The door opened and my name was called, as if there were other people waiting. We went back to the area where they prepped me for the scan. I lay on a bed and they started an IV. The lady that called me back told me that I could stop drinking that "early morning delight." She did her part of the prepping routine and a guy came to take her spot. He handed me another cup full of that stuff. I quickly let him know that I was told I had had enough...he didn't agree and I had to continue drinking.

It came time for my "support group" to go to the waiting room. I was told that I needed to relax in the dark for 45 minutes and that required no talking. I just laughed. Right. Relax for 45 minutes. Was that possible? I was able to close my eyes, but my mind was racing at a very high speed. I was trying to think happy thoughts, but how happy could they actually be? Within the last three weeks, I basically died from asthma and was told that I had cancer. I was in the middle of the staging process. I had many questions and unfortunately very few answers. Happy thoughts were very difficult to come up with at that time.

The PET scan technician came and walked me to the scanner. He told me to lie on the bed. I found that funny because when I lay down, I lay on a board and not a bed. I told him that I wanted my "support group" in the room with the technician. He went and got her from the waiting room. At that point, there was another lady that came and took his spot. She was now running the machine. The wonderful thing about that was that my "support group" was able to talk through the intercom to me while I was in the scanner. That definitely helped calm my amped-up nerves.

The scan took approximately 40 minutes. As soon as it was over they said that the oncologist would be in contact with me "shortly." Since that was Friday, I knew I was going to have to wait until the *very* least the following Monday to hear anything. The next three days were some of the longest days of my life. My mind generally goes from good to absolutely horrible in about .03 seconds. Throughout the next couple days, I had thought of just about every different type of scenario that could possibly happen.

The clinic had called and wanted to schedule an appointment. I anxiously awaited the day. She had informed me that we didn't have to do any treatment as of yet! Thank you Jesus! I thought that meant that the original pathology report had somehow messed up and I was cancer free or, better yet, that Jesus had healed me.

I will address the results in a later chapter (clearly I did this on purpose so you *have* to continue reading to find out the results). Yes, I shared some of my emotional reaction here, but this was more of just retelling the story and what had happened.

There were many nights that I lay in bed not able to sleep. There were other nights where I would fall asleep as soon as my head hit the pillow because I was so exhausted from doctor's appointments, asthma stuff, and just doing everyday life. There were nights where I cried myself to sleep (don't try to deny it. We have *all* done it). But in the darkest times of our life, God knows. God knows how bad life can hurt. Does He always make it stop? No. But He does have a way of giving us peace in the storm.

Chapter 9

THE ROAD TO MORIAH

Faith is the art of holding on to things in spite of
your changing moods and circumstances.
—*C.S. Lewis*

The Bible is filled with inspirational stories. I love to read about the miracles that were constantly happening in the Old and New Testament. In the red-letter edition, it seems like every other page in the New Testament is Jesus telling some parable that can help us in real-life situations. I love reading about how Jesus opened the blinded eyes, healed those with leprosy, and raised people from the dead. But we don't really know that much about what happened during all of those sick days that preceded the healing. What about all of those lonely nights that were spent away from the family since the patients with leprosy had to live in a colony outside of town? What about the parents who had to raise their child and had to teach him/her to live without the ability to see?

When I think of amazing stories that have a massive dynamic miracle that takes place, I think of Abraham and Isaac. But it's not too often that I think of "the in-between." I am assuming that you know the story, so I am not going to get into all of the details.

We know that Isaac was Abraham's promise—not only his

promise, but his promise from God. Maybe you have a personal promise from God. Either it has already come to pass or you are holding on to it. Maybe you were told that you were never going to have children, but God said otherwise and now you have a beautiful child from God. Or maybe you received your promise from God, but He decided to take your promise away and it caught you off guard. Confused doesn't even begin to explain how you feel. What about abandoned? Betrayed? After all, how could God take your child away? Or at least make you and your baby go through the dark valley of Moriah. If you fall into that category, then you might be able to relate to Abraham a little more than I do.

Several years ago, I applied for the graduate program for the Clinical Mental Health Counseling program at Corban University. I was chosen to participate in a group interview with about eight other potential students. One of the applicants, who would end up being a classmate of mine, and I were the last two to be interviewed. We sat in a classroom together waiting for the door to open and for one of our names to be called. We started talking and she noted that her son had been diagnosed with leukemia a number of years earlier. Immediately that caught my attention. Just with that statement I could tell that this was another kindred spirit of someone who had also walked through a dark and uncertain valley.

This is my friend's story:

> February 7, 2006. This was "D-day" for our family—diagnosis day—the day our world turned upside down. Nothing in life can ever prepare you for finding out that your four-year-old son has leukemia. However, what mother has time to give in to the shock and grief when her baby needs her to absorb loads of medical information and act quickly in order to save his life? At least this is how it was for me.
>
> My son, Connor, had a fever. I assumed it was some sort

of virus—one that he would get over quickly. The only odd part was there were no other symptoms. After a week I was concerned and called the doctor. I was told to keep a lookout for purple spots. I wasn't quite sure what to make of this, but I had heard news reports about meningococcal so I figured this was the concern. Three hours later, tiny purple spots began to appear on my son's chest. It seemed he was getting paler by the second. I called the doctor again and was told to come in immediately. The doctor said he had never seen a sicker boy come through his doors. Whatever was wrong was getting worse fast. After a series of tests that were expedited through the lab, the doctor called me to his office while a nurse occupied my son. This was not a reassuring sign. Something must be really wrong and I was going to hear about it alone! (My husband had stayed home to take care of our almost-two-year-old rambunctious boy.) The doctor was at a loss for words. He finally said, "I don't know how to tell you this, but your son has leukemia." Silence. *Not computing, but I know it's bad.* Somehow my emotions automatically shut down. Fear was shoved out of the way. The reality that my little boy had cancer was stored away to be processed later. My brain clicked back on in high gear. "Ok," I said, "tell me what I need to do."

The next two weeks we lived life at Doernbecher Children's Hospital. The reality slowly began to sink in between all the pokes, procedures, tests, doctor's explanations, and sleepless nights. We were beginning a three-and-a-half year journey of chemotherapy that would change us forever. My pleading prayer was that my son would survive. To be 29 years old and already facing the mortality of my child sent me on quite the journey. One thing I knew to be true in all of it was that God was present with me. Mornings were extremely hard in the hospital. There was a moment each morning when I'd first wake up that hope existed that these horrible circumstances were just a nightmare. But then reality would sink in once again and despair would linger at the door. As I would take a shower each morning and let the tears flow (the only place my son couldn't see me cry), a song played in my head. I believe God delivered it to my heart to remind me of the truth. The lyrics are "The steadfast love of the Lord never ceases. His mercies never come to an end. They are new every morning, new every morning; great is thy faithfulness, oh Lord. Great is thy faithfulness."

My worst memory of the entire journey took place in that hospital room. My son was tormented by the pokes, constant replacing of IV lines, and all the tape that covered the sites. His skin was beginning to bleed from all the tape removal. After another IV line stopped working, the nurses had to begin the entire process of ripping off the tape, finding another vein, and hooking up all the lines again. Connor was at his limit and was kicking and screaming. The nurses asked me to help hold him down. As I held his shoulders to the table and put my face close to his to offer what comfort I could, I saw the look of betrayal in his eyes as he looked up at me with a face contorted in pain and asked, "Mommy, why are you letting them hurt me?"

My heart broke. It took years for the nightmares from that single question to stop tormenting me at night. However, in that moment on the hospital bed, God once again came near to both my son and I. As I looked in his innocent face, I responded, "Oh honey, Mama would take all these pokes for you if I could. I know it hurts right now and it's ok to cry. But it is very important for the doctors to do this. You are very sick and even though these pokes hurt, they will make you better. You can't get better without this. Can you trust me? Because I'm your mommy I would *never* let them do something to you that hurt if it wasn't to help you. I would fight them off like crazy!" His child heart was able to receive this truth and take his mama's words in faith. The funny thing was I "heard" my Heavenly Father saying the same things to me that I was saying to my son: "Will you trust me with your son? Can you believe me when I say I work things together for the *good* of those who love me? I am *for* you, not against you. I will bring beautiful things out of this tragedy—for you, your son, and others you will never meet. Can you trust me?"

That day something shifted in my heart. Just as I knew what was best for my son and was willing to let him suffer because I knew healing would result, I began to understand to a new degree that the God in whom I trusted (though I was struggling at the moment) knew what was best for me and my son. Perhaps He was willing to let us suffer because He knew that the deep and beautiful parts of our soul that live eternally are shaped, molded, redefined, and refined through the process of grief, pain, and yielding. A new kind of hope began to bloom in my heart—one that was not restricted to my present circumstances but actually transcended them.

I can't say everything changed for me that day. I struggled mightily through the process. I vented my anger at God and screamed at Him and questioned Him at times. I had a sense He was big enough to handle it. Eventually the "whys" of childhood cancer morphed into "what nows" as I began to accept the journey our family was on. I also battled depression and began to see a counselor and went on medication for a time. Sometimes no matter how hard you try or release concerns to God, the imbalance of chemicals in the brain caused by trauma and/or extreme stress can only be rectified by medication (or a miracle, if He so chooses). Ever so slowly I began to feel like my feet were back on solid ground and the mystery of the "new normal" was uncovered.

It's been over 10 years now and I'm still in the process of allowing the hard parts of life to grow my faith, release my unhealthy holds on earthly things, and help me walk in a peace that surpasses understanding. I got the answer to my prayer in that my son survived. He's had very little side effects from the chemotherapy. He will be starting high school this year and is one of the biggest and strongest kids in his class. At fourteen he is 6'1", plays basketball, and is enrolled in honors classes. What is more important, however, than all these physical successes is that his journey through cancer softened him to the plights of others around him. God used his suffering to bring about gentleness, compassion, empathy, and kindness in this young man. In addition, Connor faced many fears through treatment. For years he struggled with anxiety and fear of the unknown. However, as he has walked through them, they have become markers to him of God's faithfulness and that with God's help he can conquer his fears and live victoriously. A confident man is beginning to emerge that is able to face fears head on and walk out in faith. Life is now an exciting adventure for him. These are just some of the beautiful things that God has brought out of the ashes of childhood cancer. No matter our circumstances, our family likes to boldly proclaim the words to a song that say, "I'm no longer a slave to fear. I am a child of God." This would not have been possible without the darkness and struggle that came first.

A word that comes to my mind: sobering. To some reading this story, you might think this is a great story of faith and trust in God. I also would agree, but just like Abraham, this family didn't know that there would be a positive ending. They didn't know if they would wake up the next morning with a son who was still alive or not. Just like God wanted Abraham to trust Him with Isaac, so He wanted this mother to trust Him with her son.

Is there something in your life that God is trying to get you to trust Him with? Maybe you lost your job and you are stressing out about how the bills will get paid? Perhaps your spouse just walked out on you and you are left to raise two children on your own? Or could it be that you just got off the phone with your doctor and the news is less than stellar? What do you do? How do you survive? How do you force yourself to put both feet on the ground in the morning and go on with life? I don't know. I have been trying to find the answer to complicated questions such as these for years. However, one answer that I have come up with is found in Ephesians 6:13: "...and after you have done all to stand, stand..." (NIV). I may not know all of the detailed answers to life's perplexing questions, but I do know that as hard as it may be—keep on living life.

During that long walk after Abraham had gathered his son and his servants together, I imagine that he was very quiet. Perhaps Isaac was skipping along the pathway and playing with the sticks and rocks on the road (I actually don't even know how old he was). Even during all of the seemingly endless questions that children ask on road trips, I just see Abraham nodding his head in agreement to his son even though he probably wasn't really hearing him. Abraham could have been wondering why on earth he was having to go through such a difficult trial. But instead of coming up with a million reasons as to why he couldn't sacrifice his son, he came up with one reason as to why he would—because God asked him to. End of story.

Chapter 10

BREAK A LEG…OR A FOOT

We must meet the uncertainties of this world
with the certainty of the world to come.
—*A. W. Tozer*

Some of you might be reading these stories and be thinking, "Are you serious? How in the world does she call that suffering? My dog has suffered worse than her!" But hurt and pain are things that are unique to each individual. What might be hard for me might not even phase you. The level of intensity shouldn't even matter. If I know my brother or sister are hurting, then I too will hurt.

Towards the end of November 2009, something unexpected happened. My parents were on a week-long cruise and I had the house all to myself. It was vacation time for all of us! They left on a Friday and wouldn't return for about 10 days. Yes, that is right, 10 days with me being home alone! To say I was excited would be an understatement.

That Sunday I spent the afternoon at my church. We had a Spanish group that would use our fellowship hall during the afternoon. Of course, Spanish church music is predominately fast and has a catchy beat. I was doing some work in the back and I was walking down the hallway. Randomly, I decided to jump and "dance to the music." I jumped one time and when I landed, my whole body crumpled to the ground. Up to that point, I couldn't remember how long it had been since I had been in so much pain.

The funny thing is that I couldn't stop laughing. The situation was pretty funny because one of my friends had watched it happen. I tried to stand up after a while and my foot hurt like it was the end of the world. I used the wall as support and walked into the sanctuary. I sat down in the nearest seat available. I started to get dizzy and wondered how I could have hurt my foot so badly. I wasn't doing anything crazy, nor was I wearing heels.

I sat down until church started and I hobbled my way over to my normal seat. I had a couple people flippantly telling me to stop faking since I was limping pretty bad. But I assure you, there was no faking involved. I was supposed to be playing the drums that night, but I couldn't even move my foot, much less play the drums. By the end of service, my foot was three times its normal size and was turning a very attractive shade of blue and black.

I hobbled out to my car and drove home. I was hoping that by the morning the swelling would go down so I could go to college. I was still able to walk, but it took me a long time to get anywhere. Unfortunately, my bedroom was upstairs in the house that we were living in during that time. In order to get upstairs, I had to crawl like a little toddler. This was one of the times I was thankful that I was home alone.

I got up the next morning hoping to be able to go to school. No such luck. My foot looked worse than the night before. My sister ended up coming over and taking me to urgent care. The doctor took one look at it and ordered x-rays right away. She came into the room about five minutes after I was returned from getting the x-ray done. She said, "So you broke your foot. Here is a list of podiatrists and a boot for you to wear along with some crutches." Talk about heartwarming sympathy.

She left the room and I just sat there in frustrated silence. Broke?! How could my foot be broken?! I didn't even do anything! And to top it off, my father was on a cruise where I couldn't just call him on the phone. I had to be the grown-up. I had a huge lists of podiatrists. How on earth was I supposed to know which one to call? So I did the only thing that I could think of. I started from the top and worked my way down. The second on the list had an availability that week. I booked the appointment. I officially felt all grown up. I was used to making normal doctor appointments, but this was a foreign process for some reason.

The day came for the appointment and I was sure that they were just going to put a cast on it and take it off in six weeks. Seemed easy enough.

I made my way to the third floor of the building via the elevator. I signed in and was taken to get a more accurate x-ray done. The new doctor walked in and introduced himself. I quickly knew that I had made the right decision when choosing him—not because of his extreme medical competence, but for the fact alone that he was *very* attractive. I realized that was probably the dumbest move on my part because he would be dealing with my feet, and we can all imagine what feet smell like after being in a boot or cast for a while. But he assured me that no matter how bad my feet looked/smelled that he had seen/smelt worse. Clearly I felt comforted (not).

I was fine with going to the doctors alone because I thought it would have been a rather easy process. However, when he started talking I realized that I had NO idea what I was doing. One of the first things he said was that I needed to have surgery. *Surgery!?* "Excuse me, sir, but I think you got the files mixed up with one of the patients in the waiting room. Don't worry, I won't sue you or anything. It was an honest mistake."

He just laughed and assured me it was no mistake. I even made him show me the file so I could double check my name and date of birth. Everything was correct. I had to have surgery. I didn't want to think too much about it because the thought of "going under the knife" terrified me. But I was never going to tell anyone that. After all, it was just a little procedure, right? All they were going to do was drill a couple screws in the bone—simple enough.

Since I went to the appointment alone, I had to schedule the surgery date (as if it were my choice). He gave me two dates that would work. The only one that would work for me was five days before Christmas. Wonderful. I already had a trip planned to go to the east coast the week prior to the surgery and there was no way I was going to cancel. Walking through airports on crutches was annoying. Walking through airports with crutches *and* asthma was...signing my death wish (or so it felt like).

I finally realized that I could just call customer service and someone would push me in a wheelchair. Unfortunately, that was at the end of my trip so I only got to take advantage of that one time.

I returned home on Wednesday night and had to be at the hospital at 7 the next morning. Something I had known but didn't want to face was that I wouldn't be able to play the drums for at *least* another 3-4 months. When I got home, I called my friend at 10 pm to come pick me up and take me to the church. I played the drums for almost two hours. Who knows if I would even make it out of surgery alive (clearly being melodramatic)?!

The next morning came and I was dreading it. However, I knew this needed to be done and I did it. It was just an outpatient surgery, so I didn't need anything for overnight. My grandparents had shown up just in time and we said a quick prayer. The anesthesiologist came into my room to start prepping me for surgery. He warned me when he was about to put the stuff through the IV. I was talking normal and then all of the sudden I stopped. My eyes opened up real big and I said, "Wooooahhhhhh!" I officially knew what being high felt like.

We rolled into the operating room and I would not shut up. I kept on rambling about absolutely nothing. The first thing I questioned was why on earth it was so cold! I was shivering and was pretty sure that I was going to die from hypothermia rather than the surgery itself. And I was supposed to trust these doctors that were cutting into me?! Great.

They informed me that they are used to it and love the cold. They said that they keep it so cold so the room can stay sterile and kill potential germs.

They strapped my arms down and I remember feeling *very* uneasy about that. I was going in and out of consciousness throughout the surgery. I had an oxygen mask on and one of the times that I woke up I remember my nose itching. Just one problem. My arms were strapped down. Oh great. So I got the anesthesiologists attention. He lifted up the mask and I said, "My nose is itching!" He just replied with, "Um. Okay." Okay?! That is all you are going to say!? I looked him in the eyes and said, "So can you scratch it?! What do you think I am paying you for?" Clearly people do some crazy things when they are not thinking clearly.

About halfway through the surgery, I woke up again. This time I could hear something, smell something, feel something, and see something. Wonderful. I woke up when the doctor was drilling through the bone. I felt the pressure and could see the smoke. I started to move my leg and the drill stopped. The doctor calmly said, "Amber. Please stop moving." I quietly said, "Well, then give me some more drugs so I can go to sleep." Within about 10 seconds I was out!

Before I knew it, I was in recovery. On morphine. Lots and lots of morphine. I don't even want to know all of the things I said while being pumped full of pain killers. I am sure the nurses and doctors had a great time.

Eventually I was "released" and was getting to go home. Hours turned into days. Days turned into weeks. Weeks turned into months. During one of my checkups, I was walking with my crutches and a lady in the clinic stopped me. She said, "I am flabbergasted! Out of everyone I have seen use crutches, I have never seen anyone use them as ladylike as you are!" I was shocked! I don't think I have ever been called "ladylike" and definitely not on crutches! But I took the compliment and wore it proudly. . .for the next two minutes at least.

I got on the elevator and hit the main lobby button. I started to go down and all of the sudden the elevator stopped and the fire alarm started going off. Are you serious? Not only do I not like elevators, I especially don't like being trapped in small spaces. I forced myself to stay calm. What was going on?! Was the building on fire? Was it an accident? Were they just having a fire drill? I think not knowing was the hardest part.

Finally, they got me to the second floor where I had to get off and hobble down a couple flights of stairs. At that point I didn't really care about the stares; I was just glad to be out of the elevator. Since then, if I am in an elevator and it has stopped and the doors don't open right away, my heart starts racing. This is when I use some of my handy dandy grounding techniques that I have learned from my studies in counseling.

The day came when I was scheduled to get my cast taken off. Again, I was home alone. Unfortunately, that was also during the time when the whole city was a sheet of ice. But I didn't care. As long as the clinic was open, I would somehow make a way to get there. My friend came and picked me up and took me.

They took the cast off and of course I had to take a couple of pictures before they wrapped it up again. The plan was to wear the boot for another 4-5 weeks. Those weeks came and went. I was doing well. I took everything off and started walking like a normal person... or so I thought.

Apparently, from not using my left leg for months, I had built a ton of muscle in my right leg and had almost no strength in my left leg. That was fun.

After a short while, my foot started to really hurt, and it was starting to get tender around the incision site. I made an appointment and we got new x-rays.

The doctor apologized but informed me that I had to go in for emergency surgery. The screws were starting to come out. I had *no* problem with doing this one more time, since I was in so much pain. The bone was able to heal, so all he had to do was go in and take the screws out.

This time I had a different anesthesiologist. I remember lying on the operating room table talking to him. I looked at him and said, "You are sooooo *hot!*" I thought to myself, *Amber, what in the world are you doing?!* Talk about embarrassing.

Recovery this time around was much quicker and smoother. I had to be in the boot for about another 4 weeks. I just had four more weeks and I would be back to normal. I was so relieved. During those weeks with only one good leg/foot, I began to understand how much I took for granted. I didn't realize how awesome it was that I had two good feet…until I only had one good foot.

Through this whole experience, the hardest part for me was not being able to play the drums. I am one of two main drummers in my church, and so the other drummer had to play for months with no break. When I was finally able to play, I asked him if he wouldn't mind me playing several services in a row and he was more than happy to give it up.

People have said to my face that drums are just noise. When this happens, I generally do one of two things. I either immediately walk away because I get so irritated, or I will vocalize my opinion in the calmest voice I possibly can. To me, drums are not just noise, it's a passion and a ministry. When I was about 11 years old, God started giving me this talent and ability. I definitely had to work at it, but it was there. I did not have a musical bone in my body. I couldn't sing on key. I couldn't clap on beat. There was nothing. I remember I prayed a very simple prayer (thankful God didn't overlook this one) and told God that if He were to give me this talent that I would only play for church purposes. I also gave Him the permission (as if He needed it) to take it away if I started doing my own thing.

Anyway, playing the drums is my form of worship. I don't just play because our church needs a drummer. I don't just play because it's the "cool" thing to do. I play because it is the best way I know how to express my love to God. I play because it is *my* form of worship.

So all of those months without playing was very hard. By no means is that the only way I can worship. But that became my way of life for so many years and then all of the sudden it just stopped. I knew I was going to eventually play again, but that was a temporary loss that I had to work through. I didn't really talk to others about it because I didn't feel that other people could truly know what I was going through. I didn't think that anybody could understand my pain.

I had to change my way of thinking. I had to find different ways when I could see that there were actually people who did know what I was going through. There was this lady I knew that had a fantastic voice. You could hear her above everyone else (that was a good thing). She had the voice of an angel. She started having problems with her voice and wasn't able to sing for quite some time. I started to think about how she was feeling. Singing was one of her ways of worship and then all of the sudden she couldn't sing. I think there are times when we don't really appreciate what we have until it is gone. We love to worship God in our unique way, but we might not really know how precious it is until we can no longer worship using that specific.

As I mentioned earlier, most of the people that I work with have substance abuse problems. They became addicted to drugs in their early teens and have led a life full of addiction up until their 50s or

60s. I was struggling with finding a way to identify with them or truly understand what they are dealing with. My supervisor told me that I can still understand what they are going through even though I have never done drugs. Addiction is about the concept and not necessarily the "drug of choice." I used to be addicted to caffeine, even though that is a smaller pull, so I can relate to them on the level of needing something for your physical/psychological self.

This is something that I *still* have to think through often. It seems like no one could possibly understand what I am going through. There are probably times when there might not be someone who completely gets it. But I think more times than not, if I were to just look around then I would be able to find someone who understands. Sure, their circumstances probably won't line up directly to mine, but it isn't about the exact circumstances per se. I think it is more about the concept or idea.

I used to get so irritated at my high school teacher. I would be stuck on a math problem and she would constantly tell me that it is all the same. All of the math problems in the lesson are the same. What? Um, no. Clearly, she had never done math before. She would say it is the same formula, just different numbers. All I had to do was plug in the different numbers. I never understood that and I would get so frustrated...until I became a teacher. I quickly found myself saying the exact same things to my students. Of course they disagreed with me and told me I was crazy.

I feel that this is similar to life. I think that I am the ONLY person who is struggling in a specific area. But in reality, there are many people that are struggling the same way. I might have different "numbers" in the formula, but it's the same formula: loss, grief, and hurt.

CHAPTER 11

WELL, THAT'S DEPRESSING

If you're going through hell, keep going.
—*Winston Churchill*

Depression. Such a hard word to digest. It's also a word that is highly stigmatized throughout the church. If you have done any type of studying about grief, you probably would have heard about the five stages of grief: denial, anger, bargaining, depression, and acceptance. It's okay to go through depression. Dare I say that it can even be considered healthy in some instances.

I went through a difficult time with depression. I had just received a medical diagnosis that was less than stellar. Apparently, my airways can completely fill up with mucus and I could stop breathing, with no warning. Yeah, I would say that is less than ideal. I denied that I was going through depression because that seemed like such a big word. I always associated depression with not wanting to get out of bed, not wanting to see anyone, and feeling hopeless.

But that wasn't me. I had an even bigger drive for life than I did prior to the diagnosis. I wanted to conquer the world. But at the same time, I was overcome with this intense feeling of...sadness. I had to figure out a new way of living. So I was confused and I didn't believe I was going through depression. But I was.

I sat down at my computer and did a journal entry after finding out some news. It was hard. I won't lie. I have faith that God will heal me, but at the same time, what definition of healing is that referring to? Maybe getting my healing will mean that I will be in Heaven with God, only to feel no more pain on this earth. If that is the case, then I am okay with that as well.

My mind has gone wild with scenarios. Driving to get ice cream with my niece and all of the sudden I can't breathe…walking on the beach during sunset and all of the sudden I can't breathe…sitting with a client as they are exposing the deepest part of their heart and all of the sudden…. How does one learn to live with that as being a very big possibility and that becoming the new norm? I don't know. I am trying to learn though. I never really understood the statement, "We live one moment at a time" until this year.

I was given an advanced directive to fill out. I just sat there staring at it…dreading the need to start writing. How on earth was I supposed to decide how long I want to be put on life support? Do I want to be on tube feeding for two weeks? Or three weeks? When do I want the medical professional to pull the plug? While other people were deciding if they want whole milk or low-fat milk in their coffee, I was sitting there deciding how long I want to be on life support before pulling the plug.

I just sat there. Staring into empty space. *I can't do this. I am too young. I have way too much living to do.* But so did the young teenager that got hit and killed by a drunk driver. So did the little baby that just lost his life to cancer. So did the new mother who died during childbirth. We can't control when we die. I realized that somehow, someway, I needed to complete this daunting task. My professor offered to sit with me as I filled it out. It took a while, but I did it. It was hard, but it was done. I got the necessary people to sign it. Everything was done. It became an official legal document.

I loved the idea of setting new goals and crossing things off my bucket list. But not all depression is the same. There is depression, and then there is clinical depression—two very different things. My friend has been going through clinical depression for a number of years.

This is my friend's story:

> Being an individual who deals with depression is bad enough—being a Christian who fights depression on a daily basis takes it to a whole new level. I've heard it said time and time again that people who struggle with depression need to just get over it. Speaking as one who has dealt with depression for a long time, it is way easier said than done. I have seen scans of a healthy brain being compared to a brain of one who deals with depression; there is a noticeable difference between the two. One brain is full of light spots (the one without depression) where the other brain (the one with depression) shows dark patches throughout.
>
> What is it like to struggle with depression? I am so glad you asked. Let me give you a quick look into the life of someone who battles depression....
>
> It's morning. The sun is shining through my window as if trying to convince me that today will be different—better. I put the pillow over my head and try to convince myself that life is still worth living—that, eventually, this battle will be over and the light will somehow pierce through my darkness and make me thankful I kept on fighting. But who am I kidding? Do I really believe that day will ever come? No.
>
> I am existing in a dark abyss of trying, every day, to claw my way toward the top where the light is known to be. I have fallen so far down into the darkness, I can't even see the light anymore, but I know it's up there...somewhere. I am sick and tired of focusing all of my energy on something that might not ever happen...having the ability to wake up

with a real smile on my face. I would rather die than live. I have no desire to do anything anymore. I live, every day, wishing I were dead. I have thought a lot about death. In my depression, I have thought about death way more than I have thought about life.

I've focused my whole life on building up walls so that others can't see what is really happening beneath the surface. On the outside, I appear like everything is going great. I have learned to exist in a way that is acceptable to everyone. If someone needs to laugh, I will crack jokes until they're laughing. If someone needs to cry, I will cry with them so they don't feel so alone. If someone needs support, I will be as supportive as I can possibly be. But inside, I am dead.

Being depressed does not necessarily mean one is suicidal. People can be depressed without being suicidal. Chances are, however, that if someone is suicidal, then he/she is battling depression. Some signs that someone is considering suicide include things like going from sad to being very calm or appearing to be happy, always talking or thinking about death, clinical depression (deep sadness, loss of interest, trouble sleeping, and eating) that gets worse, putting affairs in order (tying up loose ends, writing letters, etc.), saying things like "it would be better if I wasn't here" or "I want out," talking about suicide, or visiting or calling people one cares about. Some people with depression also struggle with self-harm (cutting, burning, pulling out hair, etc.). A reason for that would be the individual believes he/she is deserving of punishment; with everything else in life going out of control, they feel the need to suffer from a pain that they can control. There is a "darkness" that appeals to them; there are many reasons.

I do want to say that I would not be alive today if it

were not for God. Sometimes it is hard battling depression while trying to live for God. The enemy will fill your head with thoughts of worthlessness and hopelessness. He will do everything he can to try and convince you that you are unlovable. He will torment you with everything he has to try and confuse you and make you believe a lie. That makes me think of I Corinthians 14:33: the Bible tell us that God is not the author of confusion. A challenge to you from me, if you struggle with depression/suicidal thoughts/self-harm, find scriptures that speak life into you, type them up and print them out, and hang them all over your house and read them out loud when you pass by them every day.

Life hurts. Depression is a real thing that real people go through. The psalmist, David, was a man after God's own heart, and yet I think it is very evident that he even went through depression. I used to wonder how in the world someone could be depressed. Life is too great to get depressed! But I am just like everyone else...until it happens to me. All of the sudden, I am able to understand.

I think you have been able to tell that this book is not about giving advice for what to do when these things happen; it's about awareness that these things *do* happen. It's okay if they do, or better yet, when they do. It's okay to hurt. It's okay to cry. It's okay to laugh. It's okay to mourn. It's okay to grieve. However you feel, it's okay. But know that you are not alone. Even though depression might not be a topic that people talk about around the dinner table, it is still something that is experienced by many people. There is hope in hopeless situations.

I was going through a grieving stage several months after I filled out the advanced directive, but I had so many big projects I was working on and I knew I had to be on my "A" game. I decided to completely ignore the emotional pain of my physical limitations.

For a month I did great! I didn't cry one tear over it. And all of the sudden, out of nowhere, it felt as though I was slammed against the wall. Would that have happened if I had not ignored everything? If I hadn't twisted the lid so tight on my grief, maybe the pressure wouldn't have been so strong.

Depression is something that people don't want to talk about. Instead, depression should be held in the light where it can breathe and be heard and healed instead of hidden. No matter what stage of the grieving process you are in, Jesus loves you. I know that sounds like a cliché, but it's true. Jesus loves you.

Chapter 12

THE WAITING ROOM

Worry does not empty tomorrow of its sorrow.
It empties today of its strength.
—*Corrie Ten Boom*

have never really liked waiting rooms. I have spent more than enough time occupying one of those uncomfortable chairs. Waiting rooms are generally filled with sick people. Great. Just where I want to spend my time—in a room full of other sick people. Yes, I do like being around other "sick" people because they "get" me more than those who are not sick, but not in the waiting room. Waiting room people seem to usually be sick with a cold or flu; many are sneezing and wiping their hands on anything and everything.

I remember one specific waiting room. This experience took place about six months after my original cancer diagnosis. I went to my oncology clinic for an appointment. This was my first time going completely alone. I have been to medical appointments many times by myself, but never oncology. I walked in and checked in at the desk. The waiting room had several different "stages" of people. I sat in the first vacant seat that I saw. Right behind was an older gentleman. He was talking to someone else that was sitting next to him. This man said, "I just talked to my doctor and they said there is nothing they can do. It is just a matter of months." I sat still in my chair and couldn't move.

There was another lady who had just recently been diagnosed with cancer and who was waiting for her first infusion. She was waiting with her husband and was clutching onto her purse like it was a security blanket. The door opened and the oncology nurse said, "Amber?"

It took a second for it to register with me. I was in a room full of cancer patients, but I didn't identify myself as one. Those waiting rooms were the hardest. I was literally watching life being drained out of people as we sat there waiting for our turn.

While some waiting rooms are okay, some waiting rooms are generally associated with pain. We go to the doctor because we are sick (or for regular checkups). We go to the counselor to get help (or just for maintenance purposes). Waiting rooms are for people who need help fixing something. It order to fix something that must mean that something is broken.

We don't like the idea of being broken. We like the idea of being whole. After all, who wants to identify as being sick? Not me. I would prefer that everything be perfect.

But is it bad to be sick? Is it bad to be broken? Does it mean that something is wrong with your relationship with God?

No. It doesn't mean that you have a lack of faith. It doesn't mean that you have some deep-rooted anger that you haven't dealt with (these are possibilities, but not necessarily the answer). Sometimes it means that you are (get ready for it)…human. Sometimes life just happens. The Bible says that it rains on the just and on the unjust (Matthew 5:25). The story of Job comes to mind. David is another guy that comes to mind. And the crazy thing is that David was a "man after God's own heart." And yet he still sinned and had complications interrupt his life.

Even if you have a support group with you in the waiting room, it can seem like you are all alone. But rest assured that Jesus knows exactly how you feel. Just before He was arrested, He and his disciples went to the garden of Gethsemane. Jesus had told them to wait while He went up a little bit further. That was probably one of the hardest times of his short life. And the crazy thing is that He came back down to find his disciples...*sleeping!* He asked them to stay up and pray. But what did they decide to do?! Sleep. When He needed them the most they decided to take a nap.

They didn't understand what was going on. They weren't experiencing the same kind of mourning that Jesus was experiencing. I wonder if they were secretly irritated at themselves for not staying awake and praying with the same intensity that Jesus was praying. I wonder if that changed the way they were with friends and family after that experience.

My friend and her husband have been in the waiting room for years. He was diagnosed with Multiple Sclerosis (MS) before I was even born. I remember being a young kid when he started using crutches. I was a teenager when he went from crutches to a wheelchair. Through all of the heartache, pain, and hurt, He has remained faithful. Since He has remained faithful, he has remained faithful.

This is my friend's story:

> Our journey into chronic illness began quietly enough. His eyes began to blur multiple times a day. He and I had been married almost 10 years, and our children were five and eight years old when the resulting diagnosis of multiple sclerosis slammed into our world. We became Mr., Mrs., and MS. For the next month, I wept through every church service. The rug under our feet had been given a tremendous jerk.
>
> Ten uneventful years passed, but around our 20th anniversary, his left leg began to weaken. His walking evolved from the use of a cane to Canadian crutches. His job as a

produce clerk in the grocery store became a challenge due to the physical demands, so his boss graciously gave him a different position. He drove his scooter around the store, handing stickers and cookies to the youngest shoppers. I still wasn't prepared for the announcement that it was time for him to retire.

Overwhelmed one night by all that was going on, I went to my husband with my concerns. He quoted "Casting all your care upon him for He careth for you." Within two weeks' time, four others gave me the same verse. I wept then as I began to understand that the Lord himself would be taking care of us. Then He proceeded to do just that! He received Social Security within four months of application. The Lord provided for all our bills even though my husband was without income during those four months. This was just the beginning of God's provision for us.

Herniated disks in his neck and a six week stay in rehab resulted in Dave's first power chair. For three years he was self-sufficient at home. Two days after Christmas 2008, his grand mal seizure woke me. Seeing the blood dripping from his mouth, his eyes wide open but blank, and then our bedroom crowded with emergency personnel announced another downward turn in Dave's health. Three seizures in two hours added epilepsy to his diagnosis list. He continued to weaken during that spring and by the end of May was falling daily.

His needs continued to escalate, setting into motion doctor visits, attorney consultations, and a visit from a state case worker. Placing him into a nursing home became the only option. A tsunami of uncertainties and fears swirled around me by day and terrorized me by night. Now the rug was being yanked back and forth, and our whole world reeled. I staggered numbly through those summer days—thinking I was losing him, our home, and my job. Everything in me rebelled as I attempted to dig in my heels but was jerked forward against my will. A call to my best friend and mentor brought immediate prayer, and God answered with peace during the day and sleep at night.

So many statements I'd heard and believed all my life: God is a provider. . . . He is our Father. . . . He can be our best Friend. . . . You can trust Him. . . . He is always with you. . . . became deeply meaningful as I relearned the meaning of each of these from personal experience.

The words to the final song in our wedding were "Hand in hand we walk each day, Hand in hand, along life's way. Walking thus we cannot stray. Hand in hand with Jesus." He has been a nursing home resident for seven years. Uncertainty has become a way of life, disappointments continues to arrive, and grief intermittently slips in uninvited and unannounced, and so we grip His hand a little tighter. The three of us are still hand in hand, but instead of Mr., Mrs., and Multiple Sclerosis, we've become Mr., Mrs., and a Magnificent Savior.

I can guarantee you that when they got married and said their wedding vows, MS was not in their mind when they both agreed "in sickness or in health."

People have been in God's waiting room for pretty much ever. The concept of waiting is all over the Bible. Moses waited for 40 years in the desert. Abraham had to wait about 25 years from the time that God told him that he would be the father of many nations until the time he had his son. Simeon waited day after day after day to see Jesus Christ.

Isn't it ironic that a key concept during the Christmas holiday is that of waiting? We wait to open our gifts. We wait to give gifts. We wait in lines. We wait to get a somewhat close parking spot. Waiting. Waiting. Waiting.

Jesus knows it is hard. But He also knows it is crucial. We have to wait for the medical tests. We want the answers right now, but there is a process. The professionals have to analyze and determine what is wrong. We have to wait to hear if we get the job. We would love to be hired on the spot, but the professionals have to do a background check. We would prefer to get a ruling right now, but we have to wait for the jury to determine if the perpetrator is innocent or guilty.

After I was diagnosed with cancer, I went to the oncologist's office to talk about the game plan. She said, "Amber, you are entering into one of the hardest parts of the cancer journey." Great. My mind jumped from bad to worse to absolutely horrible. "You are now in what we call the waiting stage." Waiting. That doesn't sound like fun. I thought waiting just over the weekend was hard enough. Are we talking a month? Six months? A year even? Her reply was, "I know you're going to love me for this—I don't know. We will wait as long as it takes."

It's been years, and I am still waiting. I go religiously for checkups and extensive bloodwork. I am told that the cancer is in there, but we are just waiting for it to start spreading before we can do treatment. Of course, that added a bunch of other questions to my already question-filled mind. Isn't the idea to stop the cancer *before* it spreads? I was confused. I still am. But for some reason or another, I trust my oncologist.

Isn't that weird? I trust my oncologist and so I am okay waiting years before we do what we *might* need to do. But on the other hand, I say that I trust God, yet I don't "settle" near as quick for the "you need to wait" instructions that I do with my oncologist. Crazy, isn't it?

I go in every 6-8 months for my checkup. So far, with my results, the doctor has called back and said, "Well, we're still waiting." When they say that, that means the cancer hasn't spread, which is good. But at the same time, it means that I am a ticking time bomb and we are still waiting for those nasty little malignant cells to overtake my body. Until then, I will impatiently wait with patience. But who knows, that day may never come.

CHAPTER 13

WHY?

*Grief is like a long valley, a winding valley where
any bend may reveal a totally new landscape.*
—*C.S. Lewis*

I don't have any children of my own, but I do have a niece. She makes me smile every single time I see her picture on my phone. I am extremely proud of her, and she has already gone through too much in her short lifetime. But believe it or not, she can get on my nerves. If we are alone together, there is one question that she asks me specifically about *everything*. Peyton, can you roll the window up? "Why?" Peyton, come check out this totally awesome scratch I just got? "Why?" Peyton, it's time to get ready for bed. "Why?" Of course my answer is normally the generic "Because." On some things I will give her a direct, detailed answer, but on other things, "because" is sufficient (for me, at least).

I can't get too irritated with her because I also often ask the "why" question. Sometimes I get a direct answer, and sometimes I get "because." Even though I know deep inside that I will *never* know the actual answers to my questions, I ask them anyway. I think I find it therapeutic to sit in a dark room all by myself, crying my guts out, and begging for God to tell me why things have to happen the way they happen.

I remember being in the hospital one time for asthma, and the doctor came into my room. He told me that there was nothing more they could do and it was just a matter of time. I asked him why my body wasn't reacting to the treatment. He started using the typical medical jargon and I stopped him mid-sentence. I said, "You really don't know why, right?" He took a deep breath and replied, "No. I'm sorry, but I don't know why."

We can come up with complex educated guesses. We can come up with a hypothesis. But at the end of the day, there are just some questions for which we don't have the answer.

Why do some people choose to get divorced? Why do people have to get cancer? Why do good people die and bad people live? Why do people kill other people? Why do people discriminate towards other people just because they are "different"? Why do parents choose drugs over their kids? Why do some people never have trouble with cars while other people are continuously pouring money into theirs? Why can some people eat a million pounds of food and not gain an ounce, but I just *look* at chocolate and automatically become obese? Why do incredibly healthy people suddenly keel over with a heart attack? Why do people fall asleep crying because they feel all alone? Why does life have to hurt?

I have an answer to those questions: I have no clue. Some of those answers could be boiled down to relational dysfunction, but that still doesn't necessarily answer them. Life just happens. I don't know why.

Why do I have to go through these medical valleys? Why do I have to be the one given a "death sentence?" Why can't it be someone who doesn't even want to live? Why can't it be someone who doesn't enjoy living and accomplishing dreams as much as I do?

It doesn't take me very long until I start thinking of someone who is dying of stage-four cancer—or perhaps someone who is in the last stages of ALS—or someone who just escaped a very dangerous relationship—or someone who just had a funeral for their two-year-old baby.

All of the sudden, my life looks pretty good. At least I have been able to live 25 years thus far. At least my body isn't being eaten from the inside out. At least my nervous system is still functioning.

I know that we aren't supposed to compare ourselves amongst ourselves—but I still do. Someone once told me, "Amber, you are going through some hard stuff. Your neighbor might be going through something even more difficult, but that still doesn't mean you don't have to deal with hard stuff yourself."

Obviously, we don't always want to have our heads down. We believe that God heals. We believe that God provides. We believe that God answers prayers. And He does. But He also understands that we are human. He knows we are not perfect. He knows we will have bad days. So I think it is okay to sit back and admit that life hurts. It's okay to say, "Man. This is stupid." Believe it or not, I think at times it is even considered "normal" to question God.

"Question God? Goodness, no! I could never do that!"

Yes. Question God. That doesn't mean you are a horrible, filthy, rotten sinner. It just means that you want to know why. I have questioned God *many* times about why I have asthma. When I feel good, I am full of hope, faith, and patience. But when I am smack dab in the middle of a severe asthma attack, I can see nowhere on the horizon why on earth I have to go through this dark and lonely valley.

The psalmist, David, questioned God—many times. Psalms 10:1 says, "O LORD, why do you stand so far away? Why do you hide when I am in trouble?" This is the exact same guy that just got done singing God's praises in the previous psalm. And now here he is, basically begging God to answer him. If I could let my imagination go, I would hear David say, "Oh come on! You have got to be kidding me! Last week everything was going great, God! I couldn't have been more happy to be called Yours. But now?! Just when I need You the most, You are nowhere to be found."

I think if we were honest with ourselves, we would admit that we have probably thought this a time or two (if not more) in our lives. To put it in more modern language: "God, after the terminal medical diagnosis, I just can't seem to make sense of life. I go to You, but I don't feel any sense of reassurance that everything is going to be okay." Or what about "God, You said you would be a mother to the motherless and a father to the fatherless. But ever since my parents died I can't feel You. I don't know why You are not there. . .when you said you would be." Does that sound familiar?

My friend went through a very traumatic experience towards the middle of 2016. The unimaginable happened. It is hard enough to lose a loved one when you have warning, but what about those times where there is no warning: a child dies in a car accident, a brother dies in a swimming accident, or a mom dies of a sudden heart attack. On Mother's Day, my friend woke up and answered a phone call early in the morning from his father. His mother had unexpectedly passed away. I asked him if he could write his thoughts down for this book.

This is my friend's story:

> May 8, 2016, was the worst day in my life. It was 5:00 a.m., and I was lying in bed when my cell phone rang. I picked it up to see who was calling me and saw that it was my dad. I hit ignore because I knew that I would be calling him later to talk to Mom since it was Mother's Day. Then the phone rang again as soon as I laid it back down on my night stand. So this time I decided to answer my phone because I knew it must be an emergency. In our family, we've always had this rule that if we ignore the first call we would call at a later time, but if the phone rings immediately after, we need to pick up because it's an emergency. On the other end was my

dad asking me if I was sitting down. I replied to him, "No, I'm lying down; it's five in the morning." He said, "Mom had a massive heart attack and she's gone." I said "What!" He repeated it again. Instantly I felt numb, angry, and betrayed by God. Just 24 hours prior, my aunt (my dad's sister) had passed away and I went to bed knowing this heartbreaking news, but to wake up with this was more than I ever could expect.

My dad began to tell me what happened. Mom had been to the hospital a night or two before this happened with neck pain and the doctor said it was muscle pain so he prescribed her a muscle relaxer. He said that this would knock her out for a while but it was normal and that she was to only take it as needed. The next day she was in pain and took the pill that was prescribed. Dad said she complained about being tired and she wanted to go rest. He thought, "Great! The pill is taking effect." He helped her to bed. A few hours passed and mom woke up to great pain. She called out to dad. He went in to see what could be done. She wanted help up and said she was hungry. She asked for his help to the restroom and then she wanted to go sit at the table and have a peanut butter sandwich. While she was in the restroom, my dad made her a sandwich. He went to the restroom to check up on her, he knocked, and there was no answer. He opened the door and mom was sitting slumped over. She barely responded. He helped her to the table and gave her the sandwich. She responded with "This doesn't have pickles on it!" My dad knew something was wrong so he helped her to the truck and took her into town to the hospital. My parents lived 45 minutes from Florence, OR, in a small town called Deadwood.

Several hours passed and the nurse came out to my dad

to update him that they needed to do a few tests. The nurse left and came back shortly yelling for my dad. She said, "Get down there, the doctor needs you right now." So my dad went as fast as he could to witness the other doctors and nurses trying to save my mom's life. The doctor told my dad that when they checked mom's blood pressure it was so high it wouldn't even register. They knew that she was about to have a massive heart attack and that she would need to be flown to Eugene. They went to move her to another bed so they could move her to another room across the hall and she went into cardiac arrest. They tried to revive her multiple times, but it was no use and she passed away from a massive heart attack.

My mind went in a million different directions. My dad and I talked for a while before he had to go and call my brother and sister. We talked about how mom would want us to be in church and that that was probably the best place for us to be. So I went to church that morning not really sure of what or why this was happening, especially on Mother's Day. I don't remember much of what happened or what was preached about because it was a blur. As I sat in church, I kept asking God why he had to take my mom. Where was God? I felt and still feel betrayed; my mom was only 64. Why couldn't God let her live to be 80 or 90? Why not 100? Yeah, why couldn't she live to be 100 years old? I see other people get to have their parents live for a long time. I feel like God is mad at me or hates me. It's really hard to trust Him and believe that He knows what's best for me.

Why didn't God give me more time to have my mom around? I don't understand why He didn't give my family a sign or something to know that my mom had so much time left like He did for my family when He took my aunt, who died just 24 hours before my mom. My aunt had battled

Amber Sirstad, MA

cancer for nine years, and we were told, "Hey, you better get up here to see your aunt because she's not going to be around much longer." We were able to go see her and say goodbye a week before she passed. Why couldn't I get the same opportunity to say goodbye to my mom like that? To say "I love you" and thank her for everything?

Now I worry about my dad, and I'm learning that not only is it hard to lose a parent, on top of feeling heartache, sadness, and worry, but it's also stressful. I don't know what I'm supposed to gain from this or learn. I know the typical answers are to take advantage of the time you do have on earth or time with loved ones. Live, laugh, love. Don't worry about tomorrow. Live for today because tomorrow will take care of itself. My favorite is "Heaven is a better place." If heaven is a better place because God took my mom, what was it before? Or "Heaven needed her." The list goes on and on and those sayings as well as others seem so cliché. What really are we supposed to learn from something like this if we are to learn anything at all? My answer is, I don't know.

Yes, I know there is a God. Yes, I know He's in control. Yes, I know that death is a part of life and we are all going to face it one day. Knowing all of this, are we supposed to learn anything from it? Does God want us or expect us to learn anything from it? Or do we just expect it to happen?

Friend, there are many people who are in the same boat as you are today. Life brings us difficulties and heartaches and we are somehow supposed to make sense of it all. But how does one make sense of a situation that makes no sense? Or I suppose a better question is, *can* someone make sense of such a difficult situation? Or is this one of those situations where the only thing you can do is trust God?

I have been a recipient of those cliché comments like my friend

84

was talking about. At the end of the day, I know that people mean well. After just hearing some shocking news, people just want to help. But they don't always know how to help. What do you say in such a time of tragedy? You want to say something, but what do you say? It can seem easier to say things such as, "Heaven needed another angel," "God will never give you more than you can bear," and "Just hang in there." Yes, I know that the Bible says that God will never give us more than we can handle, but at such a time of crisis that is one of the last things that someone wants to hear. Why? Because the situation can seem unbearable.

Sometimes the best thing to do with someone facing intense grief and loss is to...just be there. When you are racking your brain and trying to figure out what to say, sometimes it is okay to say nothing at all. Being a container for someone can be more of a benefit than rattling off the top 10 quotes about grief and loss.

I heard a quote once: "The teacher is always quiet during the test." My initial reaction was, "That'll preach!" But the more I replayed it in my mind, it started settling in my spirit. I have had many tests in school that were open book. That doesn't mean that we didn't study. If you were smart, then you would study as though it wasn't open book. Because generally the tests were timed and to look through the whole book for just one answer is way too time consuming, much less repeating that process 20 times.

In real life, we have tests. A lot of tests. There are those who are considered to be great test takers. Likewise, there are those who get, what we like to call, test anxiety. Either way, you have to take the test alone. But the exciting thing is that *all* of your tests are open-book. You can open the Bible anytime you need. You can get all of the answers that you need. The best part? The Teacher wrote the Book, so He is very much aware of the content and how to apply it in today's day and age.

I used to think that when I got to Heaven I was going to take some time and ask God why certain things happened. But I recently came to the conclusion that that will be the furthest thing from my mind. At that point, it won't matter. It won't matter why I got in that car wreck. It won't matter why I had that seizure. It won't matter why my friends went through very dark times. It won't matter that I almost stopped breathing many times. It won't matter that I had to deal with the emotions of cancer. What will matter is that we are finally home. We will finally be home with Jesus. I can't remember where I read this, but it stuck out to me. Someone once said, "After death, there is something else. There is everything else. There is Jesus." So we need not fear death, for Jesus will be there.

Chapter 14

WHY ME? WHY HERE? WHY NOW?

Courage is being scared to death, but saddling up anyway.
—*John Wayne.*

I n the previous chapter, I talked about the ever-pending question, "Why?" Unfortunately, between the time I wrote that chapter and now, I still don't have an answer for you. My answer remains the same. Because. I don't know why; I just know because. Because that is how life goes. Because I didn't take care of my body. Because that person is full of self-hatred. Because…God is in control. It's hard to admit that sometimes. Why? Because. Because we look to God to save us from trouble and when we face trouble we go straight to blaming Him. So to fully admit that God is in control is a way of saying, "I trust You."

In the beginning of June 2014, something happened in my community that shook it to its core. I woke up early to head to work, which was exactly 18 miles from my house. At the intersection next to where I live, I always take a right to get onto the freeway, which is the easiest and quickest way to get to work. This specific day was different. Instead of turning right, I turned left. I had no idea why, but I felt compelled for some strange reason.

I will be honest; I was feeling irritated because I knew if I took a different route that I would indeed be late for work. But I also knew that if I didn't follow my intuition that I might end up regretting it. So I took the turn.

It just so happens that at the top of the hill is Reynolds High School. I lived within a 1-mile radius of the school. At the intersection, if you take a right then you head towards to the freeway. However, if you take a left, then you head towards Reynolds High.

I was one block away from the school when seemingly out of nowhere cop cars came flying behind me, beside me, and in front of me. I didn't think too much of it, but after I got completely blocked in by cops I realized something was happening. I parked my car and got out.

I called into work right away saying I was going to be late. Next, I called someone I knew that had a TV to check to see if anything was on the news. Nothing. I got on the Internet on my phone and refreshed the page at least a dozen times before something finally popped up. I was standing *right* in front of the school. There was an active shooter in Reynolds High.

Active shooter? *What?!* That is something that happens in other states, but not Oregon. Within minutes, SWAT was on the scene. News station helicopters were flying around. Parents were parking all over the streets and jumping out of their cars. People from the nearby houses came bolting out, still in their pajamas.

Even though I was extremely close to the school, the difference between the students inside of the school and me was that I was safe. I felt safe. I knew I wouldn't get hurt. They didn't. I was standing in the midst of parents on their cell phones talking to their kids inside. Every civilian around was either crying, panicking, or had a look of pure devastation on their face.

Nobody knew what was happening. How many innocent lives had been taken from this world? How many people had been shot? Was there one active shooter? Or multiple? Did the shooter have just one gun that would soon run out of rounds? Or was the shooter planning on going on for what would seem like eternity? Nobody knew.

I'm sure some of you have been in similar predicaments—maybe not in an area with an active shooter, but perhaps in a situation in life where you felt completely and utterly...helpless. You wanted to do something. Anything. But you couldn't. All you could do was sit, wait, and watch.

At that point, the parents, friends, and family could only watch. I am sure that if given the opportunity, some of those moms and dads would have bolted into the school with no armor, no weapon, and no clue what they were doing. But before they would even get to the door they would have been stopped by the police force. So, at that point, everyone had to stay back and trust the cops.

About 30 minutes after the scene had filled up with police, the situation was over. Well...the beginning of the situation. The shooter, a young male of Reynolds High, was dead and it was confirmed that one other student had been shot and killed.

They bused all of the students and faculty to a nearby parking lot. I, being interested of the process, decided to go and see what was happening. It was a very large parking lot, and by the time I got there, there were no spots available. So I parked illegally. But nobody cared, everyone's mind was in or coming out of survival mode.

There was a large area that was roped off. School buses would bring the children and drop them off. Once their name was checked off on "the list" and if their guardian was there, they were free to go.

I wanted a front-row seat. I knew eventually I would go into Crisis and Trauma Counseling, and so I wanted to see what I was getting myself into. I got all the way to the front and stood off to the side. As kids started coming off the buses, I started getting goosebumps as I heard parents screaming and running to hug their children. Mothers and fathers collapsed with their kids in their arms. I had never seen anything like this before, and I would be okay with never seeing anything like that again. However, in this nation's state of being, that probably won't happen.

That was a hard experience for me, even though I was on the outside, safe from harm. What would it have been like if I were on the inside? How much more of a traumatic experience would that have been for me? Much more.

Unfortunately, I have a friend that experienced it. Well, not the shooting at Reynolds High, but the shooting at Umpqua Community College (UCC), in Roseburg, Oregon. I remember exactly where I was when I heard about it. I immediately texted her and said, "Are you still alive?" I was being lighthearted, but soon realized that this was much more serious than I thought.

The following months after the shooting were really difficult for her and her family. Before I started writing this book, I knew that I wanted to incorporate other people's stories about the difficult times in our lives. Her name quickly came to the forefront of my mind. I called her and discussed the project that I was working on. I then asked her if she could somehow, someway, put her feelings, thoughts, and emotions on paper for this book. She graciously agreed.

This is my friend's story:

> October 1, 2015, is a day that will live in my memory forever. It was the first week of my freshmen year at Umpqua Community College, and I was beyond thrilled. Little did I know that just three days later my life would be completely turned upside down. You see, being raised in a small town like Roseburg, you never expect a mass shooting. But then I guess you never do. Roseburg is the kind of place where everyone knows everyone—quiet and peaceful for the most part. That all changed at 10:30 Thursday morning.
>
> I was in writing class, taking notes. My professor had been going over essay topics and rough draft due dates when

there was a loud *pop*. We all jumped. My teacher was going to open the connecting door to the other room to see if everyone was okay. Someone yelled from the back and told her not to open it. Instead she knocked on the door and yelled through. Something was definitely wrong. Then came another, and another: *pop...pop*. I could hear screaming and crying from the next room over, and the sound of tables and chairs scraping the tile floor. It was as if everything was in slow motion yet it happened so fast. Time seemed to stand still. I completely froze. I looked to my teacher, but she was already running out the door. Total and utter chaos broke out. Everyone seemed to run to the door at the same time. At this point everyone was in a total panic, pushing and shoving. But I just sat in my seat, not knowing what to do. My friend Chris across from me saw me and yelled for me to get up. I heard his words but couldn't do anything. He yelled at me again and said we had to get out. Adrenaline immediately kicked in. Everyone was trying to get through the narrow door. I remember being in the middle of chaos and turning back to look at the flimsy wooden door that connected room 14 to room 15. I can still see it so clearly. I can hear the sound of gunshots, and I can feel the fear and panic. I honestly thought I was going to die that day.

I ran down the breezeway, not knowing where to go. People were running in every direction. All I can say is it was absolute terror. Somehow I had ended up following my teacher in the campus bookstore, where five of us girls had gone with our professor. We were immediately ushered into the stock room, where we locked and barricaded ourselves in. Even from the bookstore you could still hear gunshots. I didn't want to believe that a shooter had come onto campus and done the unthinkable. I didn't want to believe that innocent lives were lost. But in reality we all knew the truth. We got a call from campus security saying there were two active shooters on campus and for us to stay in lockdown because the suspect was running to the center of campus, right where we were located.

I began to silently pray; I didn't know what was going to happen—didn't know if I would even get to see my family again. So, in the back of that bookstore while horror filled our campus, I began to make peace with myself and with God. I knew no matter what that I wasn't alone. God was always with me, and if this was my time to go, then so be it. After that, an incredible peace came over me. No, I didn't want to die, but I wasn't afraid if that's what God allowed. There were several girls crouched in the corner crying hysterically, having a panic attack. I asked if I could pray with them, and they of course said yes. I don't remember what exactly I prayed, but I do remember just telling them over and over that I loved them and that God loved them. I had peace and I wanted them to be at peace too. If we were going to die, I wanted the last thing they knew to be that someone loved and cared for them.

Those of us who were in that bookstore that day all share this special connection. Right before state troopers found us and cleared the building, we said a group prayer, embraced, and said we loved each other. We didn't know one another a mere few hours before, but by the time the entire ordeal was over, I can honestly say I loved those people.

I remember a reporter telling me later that the nightmare was finally over. But in reality, the nightmare was just beginning. The days and weeks to follow were such a blur. Reporters called constantly for the first week. Some even camped out at our church in hopes to get the inside scoop of what had happened. Life was anything but normal, with dealing with the nightmares, the flashbacks, and the anger. The anger surprised me. I had gotten out with my life, and for that I was grateful, but I was definitely not the same person that I was before. I angered easily and lashed out at those closest to me. I was hurting, and I couldn't understand why God had let me go through something that horrific. I was struggling, mentally and emotionally. Like I said, I was a different person.

I found it hard to lift my hands at church, and to even be grateful. If I said that I didn't think of quitting church, I would be lying (I am so glad that I didn't give up). At times I wished I had just died that horrific day. In a way, those who had died had it easier than those who had survived. This was something that I had to live with—something that would haunt me for the rest of my life. It wasn't until I got into counseling that things started to get better. My counselor made me realize that bad things happen to good people and that we don't live in a just world. It wasn't God's fault; it wasn't anyone's fault except the disturbed person who carried out the horrible crime. Life is not fair, and yes sometimes it hurts. But eventually that hurt will go away. Hurt and pain do not last forever. I'm not saying it was easy, because believe me wasn't. I still have flashbacks and nightmares to this day. But I can say I have peace. I'm not the angry person I once was. I can freely lift my hands and in sincerity thank God for what he has allowed me to go through, because if God didn't think I could handle it and come through the trial without breaking, He wouldn't have allowed me to go through it in the first place. So no, life is not fair and it never will be. Bad things happen to good people. That is just life. But if you have the strength and courage to look beyond the pain and tragedy, you will find just how precious and beautiful life can be. I can honestly say, I'm so thankful God spared me that day.

That day, my dear friend experienced the tragedies of life. She experienced firsthand the hurts of life. The weeks that followed, I remember seeing her face in the paper and on the internet. I was very proud of her. She chose to rise up during this traumatic crisis. She was the rock that her fellow classmates needed. But often that is the only face we, as the general public, see—the strong, the brave, the willing. During that time when she was working through this, her family, therapist, and close friends saw something else. They saw a scared little girl.

We can only be so strong for so long. Eventually, we need to get to that place where we are willing to be weak. But of course we don't like the sound of that—weak. With weakness comes vulnerability. And who wants to be vulnerable?

When I was about eleven years old, I was playing with some other kids from my neighborhood. Two other boys and I decided that it would be fun to practice our golf swing. We got a couple golf clubs and several golf balls. We took turns swinging and seeing who could get the furthest.

I was sitting behind the boy that was swinging. He looked back and informed me that I needed to move, and so I did. I moved more toward the left. And he swung. Apparently, I didn't move far enough. Life seemed to stand still for the next thirty seconds. I jumped up and we all looked at each other. I reacted immediately by putting my hands over my face. We just stood there and stared. Not really understanding what had just happened.

I moved my hands away from my face and my face looked like a fountain. . .of blood. The blood was squirting from my cheek, just like a fountain. I told the boys to go get help. They just stood there.

I yelled at them and they didn't move an inch. I finally had to take things into my own hands. I went inside the house where I was at playing and there were no adults. I went to the next house and there were no adults. My sister was in the next house, except she couldn't handle the sight of blood. I went to another house and the adults were all gone. There were no adults in the neighborhood. I went home, cleaned up the blood, got an old towel, put it on my face, and I lay down.

Some might think that is a frivolous example, but I think it fits pretty well. For the first hour I was still in shock. I couldn't feel anything. I was in no physical pain during the first little bit. But after the shock started to wear off, the pain started to kick in. Does that sound familiar? Perhaps after losing a loved one…or getting a negative diagnosis from the doctor…or losing a job. Every situation may have a longer amount of shock, but once the shock wears off, the pain can seem overwhelmingly impossible to handle. How am I going to go on with life without my loved one? How can I face life while facing death head-on every day? How can I face my family when I can't even provide for them?

Going back to the shooting at Umpqua Community College, my friend noted that from the time they heard the shots until the time they knew everything was over and they could come out, it had been three hours. For three long hours, time stood still. For three hours they didn't know if the whole entire school had been shot up. For three hours they didn't know that they weren't the only survivors. For three hours they lived in the unknown.

The unknown can be a scary place. As humans, we don't like the unknown. Why? Well, I am sure there are multiple reasons, but mainly I think it comes down to control—not control in a weird, unhealthy way, but in a normal way. We like to control our day as much as possible. Another way to view control is viewing the fact that we make decisions. Every day we decide to get up or not. We decide what we want to eat for breakfast. We decide if we want to hurry and run the yellow light or slow down. We decide if we want to let the elder lady get the close parking spot or if we want to go ahead and take it. We decide if we are willing to forgive someone who isn't even sorry or if we hold the wrongdoing against them.

Several months ago, I was spending the weekend in Seaside, OR. It was pouring rain pretty much the whole time. My friend called me and asked if I had a bumper sticker that says, "Drum machines have no soul"? I smiled and confirmed. I was told that I need to come right away because my window opposite of the windshield was broken. I had no idea what that meant. Another friend drove me to where my car was at. We pulled up and I froze. My window was not broken. My window was shattered in a million or more pieces. In addition, it had about three hours of rain in my back seat. Nothing was stolen, someone was just trying to make a statement.

That just reminded me how fast life can change. That day had been a good day...until the phone call. It only takes seconds for our life to shatter it what would seem like a million pieces.

I talked with my friend's mother briefly about that day in Roseburg. Her mom was at the local hospital and was on duty during the time of the shooting. Someone had told her that there was a mass shooting at UCC, and she described the feeling as if someone had just sucker-punched her. Think about it...what would you do if someone told you that there was an active shooter killing people left and right on the same campus that you knew your child was on at that very moment? I am sure that is one of those things where you have NO idea what you would do unless you were put in that situation. I am sure she was terrified. She had to face the unknown. Was one of the people coming to the hospital her daughter? Was her daughter even alive? She knew nothing.

In my graduate school classes, we had two guest speakers. One was on the trauma team that went down to the campus as soon as it happened, and the other was one of the people that helped during the clean up. Hearing those two people describe what had happened was unforgettable, but knowing that my friend was there, in the midst of everything, was even more...traumatizing. I had a better glimpse into what this family had gone through, but still I had no idea.

Chapter 15

ANGELS UNAWARE

If God send us on stony paths, He provides strong shoes.
—*Corrie Ten Boom*

For over a year I have been determined to go into Crisis and Trauma Counseling. God has somehow blessed me with the ability to be able to think with my head on straight while faced with a crisis situation (unless it's my own, in which case I am a wreck). There is something about the challenge of being able to stay calm while adrenaline is coursing through your body.

Several months ago, I was on my way home from a gathering that involved members of my youth group. It was probably nine in the evening. I was driving down the freeway in the right lane going about 65 mph (give or take 7 mph). Everything was going great. I was looking forward to having a nice relaxing evening at home, which is rare during graduate school.

All the sudden I saw this black sports car zoom past me…on the right side. Now I am sure you probably re-read the previous paragraph to see what lane I was in. I was in the right lane and the car passed me on the right shoulder. I had a front row seat to one of the craziest car accidents that I have ever witnessed.

The car was heading east with the rest of the traffic and then all the sudden it turned and was heading north. It was like everything was in slow motion. I knew there was absolutely nothing I could do and so I just watched with my mouth hanging wide open.

I watched as the car slammed into the barrier. The car flipped and rolled several times and started to spin around before it came to a complete stop. I cautiously slowed down. Several other cars stopped, but nobody jumped out of their cars. We were all waiting to see if the car was going to blow up. There was liquid all over the road and the car was smoking. All the sudden one of the doors opened. A man in a military outfit jumped out and started to run towards the car. That was my sign—Amber, get out and go help!

There were four other main people that got out to help, not including me. One was a military guy, two other people were EMTs that were off the clock, and another lady. I thought to myself, *Wow! These people are lucky to have such a great team to help them!* Since the medical part was covered, I identified myself as clergy/therapist in training.

The EMTs were able to get the passenger safely to the other side of the freeway. The driver was walking around and kept saying that he had no idea what had happened. Some of the spectators were saying that he clearly had a head injury because he didn't know what was going on. I, on the other hand, knew exactly what was going on. The dude was flying higher than a kite. We made eye contact and he just stared at me. I don't know everything there is to know about drugs, but I have learned enough to tell when someone is super high.

He told the firefighters that someone had hit him. They looked around and shockingly didn't find another car. I quickly jumped in to give my statement. None of the other people that stopped to help saw firsthand what had happened. I was it. Even though it appeared obvious—there was no other car involved. So clearly it was his fault. End of story.

I decided that my job there was done, and so I walked to my car and drove away. I checked in with myself to see how I was doing.

First, I checked my pulse and it was going at its normal rate. Next, I checked to see if I was still breathing (yes, that is a job I have to do), and believe it or not I was! I held out my hand to see how bad I was shaking, and I was hardly shaking at all (the shaking I was having was due to medication). I secretly had to smile at myself and was experiencing a moment where I was proud at myself. I did good and I didn't die.

It was at that moment that I pressed the rewind button in my memory and relived what had happened. It hit me that I was hugging the left side of the right lane. I generally try and stay in the middle as much as I can, or the opposite side of where cars are. So, for me to hug the left part of the lane was abnormal. But if I would have hugged the right side of the lane, the car would have plowed into me going at least 90 mph. And if that would have happened, I would not be writing this book right now. It's amazing to see first-hand the protection that God puts on our lives. It's said that everyone has a guardian angel with them. I am pretty sure that I have multiple guardian angels working around the clock...even when I am sleeping.

My friend also has the same testimony of guardian angels watching over her during a very traumatic event.

This is my friend's story:

> I arrived in Bangladesh for a short-term mission's appointment on the evening of June 30th, 2016. My first full day in Bangladesh was relaxing, light-hearted, and fun. After a restful morning of sleeping in and trying to get adjusted to a 12-hour time difference, the missionary I was staying with and some friends from the local church took me for a fun day of shopping at an open-air market. It was so enjoyable to be immersed in local culture, surrounded by colorful crowds of people, all in a hurry, all just living their lives and headed in different directions shopping, selling, and in some cases

begging. I enjoyed taking it all in—trying to absorb and fully experience this new culture in which I would be living for the next five weeks. After shopping, we even stopped at a street-side coconut stand and I got to drink fresh coconut milk out straight out of the shell for the first time. This was the life—and I was enthusiastic about this adventure that was just beginning.

Later that evening, we met some other local missionaries for dinner in Gulshan, an upscale community within Dhaka that is home to diplomats, ambassadors from foreign countries, expatriates, and most of the country's foreign embassies. We decided on a restaurant that was rumored to have a special Iftar buffet. Iftar is the evening meal, which breaks the daily fasts during the Muslim holiday of Ramadan. Many restaurants really pull out the stops and serve fancy spreads during Ramadan in celebration of Iftar. True to what we had heard about the restaurant, we enjoyed a lovely meal and then went home for the evening.

Before retiring to bed, my missionary friend and I stayed up for a bit visiting, checking our email, and discussing plans for the next few weeks. We were very excited about a team of fifty plus young people who would soon be arriving from the States to participate in and help run a youth camp for over 300 Bangladeshi youth and help with graduation commencement for the local Bible school in Dhaka. There were so many exciting things planned and so many events to look forward to. So much work, preparation, and planning was about to pay off with what we knew would be an awesome move of God and so many incredible things that would soon happen.

A message popped up on my friend's computer. "Where are you? Are you and your friend home?" it read. It was from my friend's Muslim neighbor who lived on the floor below us—her landlord. "Yes," my friend responded. "We are home and safe. Why do you ask?" That is when we found out that there was a live hostage situation occurring at a bakery in Gulshan, just a few minutes' drive from where we had just been eating dinner, and from where we had stopped at a grocery store afterwards before heading home. In fact, the bakery was only two blocks away from the home of our other missionary friends who had probably just reached home after dropping us off.

We both quickly Googled the news and started reading out loud back and forth from the articles that we found regarding the situation. Six terrorists had stormed the bakery filled with people celebrating Iftar, armed with explosive devices, sharp weapons, and guns. My friend was in shock. This was a bakery that she and the other local missionaries had recently found on a fluke. It was at the end of a dead-end street, with not so much as a sign at the street to advertise it. They frequented it often and had, in fact, booked a reservation to take the whole American youth missions team there in a little over a week because it was so nice and the food was incredible.

The two of us became transfixed as this horrific event unfolded just minutes away from us, reading update after update as they popped up on our computer screens. Our missionary friends called us, wondering if we had heard what was happening. It turns out that their 20-year-old son had three former classmate friends in the bakery. A mutual school friend was getting texts from the young people in the bakery, and was forwarding all those live updates to the missionary's son. We all prayed and continued to monitor the news...too upset to sleep, praying and hoping the nightmare would end soon. News continued to pour in. Multiple police officers were shot and were being taken to the hospital for treatment of wounds. As the hours stretched on, although we prayed for the safety of the hostages, a sickening feeling settled over us as we realized the likelihood of a good outcome was becoming very slim.

It was daytime in the states, and friends from the U.S. began messaging us. As concern from friends and family poured in, we realized what a big deal this was—that it was hitting all the big news stations across the globe and back home. It was such a surreal feeling.

Sometime in the early morning shortly before dawn, we both reluctantly went to bed, hating to go to sleep without knowing what the outcome would be...thinking of all those hostages, police officers, and our young friend's three classmates who were locked in a bathroom inside the bakery trying to hide.

Morning came, and to our surprise and dismay, the situation was still not over. Shortly before 8 a.m., our missionary friends who lived two blocks away heard a series of explosions and gunfire. After being unable to negotiate successfully, around one hundred law enforcement officers and military commandos with tanks went in, bulldozing through the front of the restaurant and engaging in heavy gunfire in a last-ditch effort to free the remaining hostages and capture or neutralize the terrorists. By around 10 a.m., the hostage situation was over. Thirteen hostages were rescued, two police officers were dead, forty people injured, six militants were killed, one was captured, and twenty hostages were dead after a 10-hour stand-off. Most of the victims had been killed execution-style with sharp weapons.

ISIS immediately claimed responsibility, but it was found to be the work of local, home-grown militants.

The days that followed were ones filled with numb disbelief. The atmosphere of the whole country could only be compared to the feeling in the United States during the aftermath of 9-II. This was on a much smaller scale, yes, but this was the biggest terrorist attack of this kind that Bangladesh had ever seen.

The attack hit very close to home, and ties were extremely personal. The son of our missionary friends lost three of his classmates: one young man and two young ladies. All three of them were home visiting family but were attending universities in the United States—ambitious, smart, studious young people with bright futures. Faraaz Ayaaz Hossain was a Bangladeshi and a Muslim. He died a selfless hero, refusing to leave when the attackers told him he could because he was Muslim. He chose to stay and try to defend his two friends. Not only was Faraaz a classmate of our missionary friends' son, but he also was his fellow boy scout when they were children, in a troupe led by our missionary friend.

A Sri Lankan couple who were friends of the local missionaries and who managed a local hotel were able to escape into the garden behind the restaurant during the attack. The garden was walled off, so they had to hide behind the bakery all night until the ordeal was over. They immediately left Dhaka after the attack and have no plan to ever return. One of the police officers killed was a friend of the pastor of the church in Dhaka and had frequently been influential in serving the church with any of their law enforcement needs.

Not only was the aftermath devastating due to personal connections with the victims, but it also drastically impacted all our plans for church events. A day or two before the American youth missions team was to leave for Bangladesh, it was decided that the trip would be canceled and they would instead have their missions trip on the East Coast. Hotels, campgrounds, restaurants, buses, and tourist events had already been booked for this trip, and deposits had been made. The difficult decision was made to postpone youth camp...a sad but prudent decision. We also decided that it would be good for all of us missionaries to leave the country for two weeks while the dust settled.

A day or two after the attack, a memorial near the site began to take shape. A candlelight vigil with thousands of people was held. Our missionary friends were both photographed and interviewed when they visited the site. Photographs of them praying and weeping and interviews with them went viral through various news outlets both locally and internationally.

The missionary's son was especially struck with grief and understandably traumatized over the loss of his friends and felt unsafe to go out in public in the very country he had grown up in and loved. Bangladeshis were grieved and baffled as to how their own countrymen could rise up and commit such a crime against people in their own country. When we visited the memorial site soon after the attack, we were interviewed by a local news anchor who echoed what we had heard from so many other Bangladeshis. He started the interview by apologizing to us that this had happened to us while in their country. The Bangladeshis' remorse for this attack on a café frequented by foreigners was evident by a sign posted at the memorial, which read: "Dear foreigners, we still have many Faraaz Bhaiyas (brothers like him), so don't lose faith in our country."

The peace of God and calm beyond my own understanding was felt throughout the entire ordeal and for the remainder of my mission's trip. However, the fact still remains—life hurts. Innocent lives of way too many people were brutally snuffed out. Plans had to be altered and canceled, bringing disappointment for a lot of young people both in the United States and Bangladesh. Bible School graduation was postponed for several weeks, because it was supposed to be a happy, celebratory event, and frankly, no one felt like celebrating. My missions itinerary had to be completely changed due to security issues. Bangladesh was left reeling and in mourning along with four other countries who lost citizens in the events of July 1, 2016.

At the time of this writing, it's still less than two months since the attack. I find myself reflecting every day on the reality that my friends and I could have died in that attack, as all three of them had considered taking me to that bakery for dinner. None of them voiced that idea, and they ultimately decided on that other restaurant that night. Life has a way of throwing situations at us that just don't make sense, and it leaves us with no escaping the fact that life hurts. . ..

My friend was telling me a quick version of this experience and all I could do was shake my head and say, "Oh my word." I can't even imagine. I can't imagine what she felt. I can't imagine what the citizens of Bangladesh felt. I can't imagine what the missionary's son felt. I can't imagine what the last thoughts of those who died that day were. But I know the One who knows exactly how they *all* felt. I know the One who can relate the best to all of them. I also know that when my friend hurt that day, Jesus also hurt that day. When we hurt, He hurts.

Chapter 16

DOES JOY REALLY COME IN THE MORNING?!

"What I am looking for is not 'out there.' It is in me."
—*Helen Keller*

As I am writing this, I am having flashbacks to my childhood. I don't know if children do this anymore, but as a kid it wasn't enough for me just to simply say, "I promise." Instead, in order for us to really mean it, we had to "pinky promise." If you dared to break a pinky promise, you were...pretty much the scum of the earth. Okay, I might be exaggerating just a tad, but I think you understand what I am trying to say. A promise is a big thing. To break a promise is even bigger.

It's one thing to have someone on earth make us a promise, but it goes to a whole other level when God makes us a promise. Likewise, it hurts when our friend breaks their promise to us. But when it seems as though God gave up on His promise, hurt doesn't even begin to scratch the surface. A better feeling word might be abandonment, intense disappointment, or even anger. Yes, we get angry at God. It isn't something that we generally stand up in church and tell the whole world about, but it's there. If we don't recognize it, then we can't work through it.

Have you ever had a promise from God? Perhaps He made you a promise and it looks nowhere near being fulfilled. The more time that goes by the harder it is to keep the original excitement and happiness that you felt when you first received the promise. I am currently 26-years-old, and I am sure that some of you are still holding onto a promise that God gave you *long* before I was born. The interesting thing is that since we are human, we are bound by time. But God has no time constraints. God does not run on a time schedule.

My friend went through a very difficult time a number of years ago. She received a promise from God but wasn't given any specific time frame. But in the midst of receiving the promise, she had to walk through a valley…a very dark, painful, abusive valley. Well, instead of a valley, more like an alley. At least in a valley you can see a way out. When you're backed up against a wall, there is only one way to get out. I am thankful that my friend was able to discover the only way out.

This is my friend's story:

> A decade of marriage lived apart more than together. Two and a half years here, three years there…gone was the time and gone was the feeling of accomplishment of reaching such a lofty goal.
>
> The last separation lasted for nearly three years while he lived and worked out of the country. Although it was a very uncertain time for my daughters and I, it was an easier time. We could be involved in whatever we wanted at church, we could be at the church when the doors where open, we could go to every conference, we could have people over; both girls were blessed to be enrolled at our Christian school! For their sake and mine, we were allowed to draw close to God and grow…under His wings.

It was right before the last time my husband came home when I fought God wholeheartedly. I pounded the ground, I screamed, I cried out to God, as He spoke into my heart that I needed to *love* my husband.... "If that is what you can call him," I sneered to God. Just as fast as the thought entered my mind, so did the marriage vows. "OK! Fine, God! Tell me why I have to *love* him when he doesn't even live here!"

If I've ever heard the voice of God, it was then, "I'm bringing him home."

The question "why" didn't even cross my mind. Just no. Nope. No thank you, God. How much nicer can I say it? I'm not interested.... Are you crazy? Do you know what he's been doing? I mean, the practical part is, what kind of habits and diseases will he bringing "home." No. Final answer is no. Followed by more fist pounding, more screaming, more tears...impossible tears that led to an impossible answer.

"Fine, God!" If you are going to bring him home, you'll have to give me a love for him because I don't want anything to do with him. I don't want my daughters around him. I hate him!

As quick as the words left me, a love like no other poured over me from the top of my head, and I felt it coming down over me and I soaked it in...all in. It was the love of God. For me. For him. For a sinner. For us all. I felt it so real, and the thoughts of all the pain, all the lies, all the distrust, left me, and only love was left. It was a true miracle.

This battle was Sunday. He called me Monday morning asking to come home. Because the love of God had already won, there was no battle on Monday.

I spent the next three and a half years learning to be the godly wife God called me to be: to love, to respect, to obey.... Even though there wasn't the reciprocal...the love the wife needs to do her part...it wasn't there. But God had asked me to do this, His love was enough. Yes, there were plenty of times I reminded God...like the time when my girls had to go spend the weekend with the Pastor's family because I was in no state to be seen...or the spontaneous long weekend trips he made...plenty of times.

It was getting bad: fights and more fights. Battles in the Spirit waged as many people were praying, battles in the car as I pumped my daughters up with the Word of God as we headed home not knowing what we would find...battles, never-ending battles.

It came to the point I could only utter prayers of, "God, thy will be done. You brought him home, filled him with the Holy Ghost, you've given him a faithful and loving family and he seems to be looking over each blessing you offered him." My real question was, "How much longer can I keep loving him and not fail God?"

It was spring 2003 when God gave me something... not necessarily "peace"...but the knowledge it was going to end. I couldn't stop it. Honestly, I couldn't even prepare for it. But I had the beginning of "peace." When God speaks, it's enough. It might not be "peace" exactly, but it is enough, just to know God has you in His hand and He knows exactly what He is doing!

It ended alright. It was ugly—so ugly. The police were called, my children witnessing it, being subjected to it, and being victims of it. Some would call this a new chapter, but this didn't feel like a beginning—only the end.

I felt grief—so much of it. Remember all that Heavenly *love* that poured over me? Well let me remind you, it was from God! The love He felt for us all to hang on that cross was given to me, for a miracle! Well, I had imagined it that way!

Was I wrong to expect a happy ending? I mean, the God of all Heaven told me to *love* him.... It only makes sense that it was for God's team, right?!

Depressed? Yes. Confused? Yes. Alone? No. I had been led by God's hand to this point. No way I was alone.

God's blessings were already working ahead of me this time. Probably the most life-changing ministry for myself, as well as youth, is Bible Quizzing. I had already been coaching our Bible quiz team since January. We were studying the book of Psalms. Even though my daughters were not quizzers yet, it grounded our family, and God's Word was alive in our home! It was no coincidence that one week after it all ended our team qualified to go to Nationals! Our summer was quickly spun into fun: fundraising, countless hours of studying, and numerous boot camps! Each one filled with scriptures that lifted my spirit.

It was all new. I was a single mom—for real this time. I was headed for divorce, and no one could stop it.

It was in the next three years where I was acutely aware that God was meeting our every need! God gave my daughters and I blessings through family, friends and strangers! Just to name a few, God gave us a home, a car, and a Christian education for my girls. I was able to work so I could finish my B.S. in mathematics at PSU, we afforded to go to Nationals every year, we were blessed to go to Landmark Conference every year, we were able to camp at Family Camp every year, and we were able to bless others by taking others along! That is the happy stuff. I'm so thankful that it was real though!

But there is the real life stuff that isn't so happy too...the stuff I don't like remembering...the visitations...the many, many pep talks on the way to be dropped off. "It'll only be two sleeps and then you'll be home." Signing their next verse cards to be memorized with little notes letting them know I loved them and was missing them while they were away.

Then there is the nightmare stuff.... The calls from your babies crying to come home only to hear a scuffle on the other end leading to, "Who are you talking to?"

Click.

He wouldn't hurt them, right? He wouldn't take them out of the country and disappear, right? Oh! They must be scared.... To my prayer closet I went.... I lived there. I had to. They needed me to. I needed me to.

Watching, experiencing, and feeling a marriage die can't be summed up to a pretty ending...it is death.

But it was through the grief that the Psalm that I had so diligently studied in 2003 came alive and brought life to me! God broke it down to five words for me, in what I soon realized were stages in my life....

Trust, Delight, Commit, Rest, Wait....Psalms 37:3-9.

For some, the stages might be longer than others. God was leading me through all the stages at one pace, but at the same time He was preparing my future husband by leading him through them too! We joke that he was in the waiting stage a long time. Maybe so, but the bottom line is we did them all and lived to tell about it!

That is why the letters, T, D, C, R, and W, are inscribed inside both our wedding rings! We are a promise and an example: You do your part and let God do the God part!

Even though you might not have gone through this exact scenario, I am sure that you can relate in some way. Have you ever been in a situation that no matter how hard you fought, it wouldn't go away? No matter how much you cried, it was still there? No matter how much it hurt, there was no relief in sight? If you could pay to just get a minute where there was no pain, then you would be willing to pay millions.

But unfortunately, that isn't how life works. We do experience pain. We do experience agony. We do experience the lingering presence of grief. It would be nice if grief would visit for just a day and then gather its stuff and head out. But it lingers…and lingers… and lingers, overstaying its welcome.

When you are surrounded with bad stuff on all sides of you, the only other thing to do is to look up. She realized that the only One that was able to help her was within her. My friend was able to find her way out of the dark alley. She still suffered the abuse. She still worried about her children during every waking moment. She was still unsure what the ending would be like. But in looking up, she made God her focal point. Psalms 121:1-2 says, "I will lift up mine eyes unto the hills, from whence cometh my help. My help cometh from the LORD, which made heaven and earth" (KJV).

My friend didn't know how long she would have to endure the abuse, but she held on to God's promise. I knew her when she was living in…dare I say a nightmare? And I know her now that she has received her promise. The transformation is beautiful. When I think of her, there is a specific verse that come to mind.

> For his anger endureth but a moment; in his favour is life: weeping may endure for a night, but joy cometh in the morning.

—Psalms 30:5

She and her husband are a wonderful example of staying faithful to God through the endless hurts, the sleepless nights, and the difficult days, only to find that joy does really come in the morning.

Chapter 17

DREAMS REALLY DO COME TRUE!

Although the world is full of suffering, it is
full also of the overcoming of it.
—*Helen Keller*

Even though the previous chapters have discussed some hard topics, when I look at my life as though I am looking into a Christmas globe, I do believe that the good outweighs the bad. I can truly say that I have been blessed beyond measure in my short lifetime.

Going after one's dreams is something that I am very passionate about. I have seen too many people in the latter years of their life live with regrets. God has given me many wonderful dreams, and I chase them with all of the energy that I have.

One of those many dreams included making my own instrumental CD. However, that always seemed far off into the future. It sounded great in theory, but to actually go through with it? How in the world could I afford it, as well as actually learn sixteen songs adequately enough on the piano? With God, all things are possible!

In November, 2014, instead of telling myself all of the reasons why I can't fulfill this dream, I asked myself, "What is stopping me from making my CD?" I thought long and hard...for about thirty seconds. I realized that there was nothing stopping me. One thing led to another and I was well on my way to making a dream come true. It took me just under a year to learn the 16 songs that I wanted.

The songs were learned and the money was raised. What now? Find a recording studio! I thought it would be super easy and the cost would basically be pennies (not literally). I was so young and naïve. I called studio after studio to find the best quality at the best price. Studios generally charge by the hour, by the song, or by the project. In addition, some studios also have a flat rate to rent the studio for a day. After those prices are added up, they charge for an engineer and/or a producer. Another additional charge that some studios add is mixing and mastering as a separate charge. Needless to say, for a split second I thought that it wouldn't be possible because my budget was way under the general cost of a studio. However, I have heard stories of miracles happening in similar situations and so I thought that if this was the right timing that God would open the perfect door. And He did.

I went and toured a recording studio. The environment was comfortable and very welcoming. The producer sounded like he knew what he was doing, so of course that made me happy. We sat down and started to talk money. In my mind I knew that I had no idea what I was doing, but there was *no* way I was going to let him see that in my face. I started out by asking him what he normally charges. He talked for a bit, but the only thing that my ears really caught was "$1,100-$1,300." It was like my mind blocked everything else out and focused on the impossible. Because that is what it was—impossible.

God specializes in situations that seem impossible to man.

After he got done talking, I clarified, "So, just to make sure, it would be about $1,200 for the whole project?" At that point, I pretty much decided that I couldn't do it because that was beyond my budget. He noted, "...per song."

Mind blown.

I was freaking out...inside. Via a miracle from God, I was able to keep myself from turning red. He asked what price range I had in mind. I went into the studio with a budget of $700. Total. How in the world could I tell him that I only had $700?! That could have potentially been a very embarrassing situation. But once again, God had my back.

I looked him straight in the eye and said, "I want to record 16 songs and break it up into two days for $700." It was almost as if time was standing still. He looked at me. And I looked at him. I honestly have no idea how much time passed before anyone spoke up. The next words out of his mouth are proof alone that God is real. He said, "Okay. 16 songs, two days, $700."

The rest is history (however, as soon as I got into my car I screamed to the top of my lungs and called several people right away).

I was trying to determine what I wanted this project to be called. Someone encouraged me and said that the title would "come to me out of the blue." I had spent so much time thinking about it and getting frustrated because nothing would come. I was standing in my kitchen doing the dishes, and out of the blue, it came to me! There was no question or doubt it my mind. My dream would be called *Hymns That Made A Difference*. In March 2016, *Hymns That Made A Difference* was released.

I knew that I wanted to do another musical project, but I had other responsibilities (such as graduating) that needed to take the forefront. I had planned on starting my next project either in 2017 or 2018. Within a month or so of the release date for my prior project, I had many people ask me when I was going to put another CD out. I realized that I didn't *have* to wait until 2017. My next project would be with me on the drums, and since that is my primary instrument I wouldn't have to dedicate as much time to practicing as I did with the piano. I had sold enough CDs to where I had enough money to start on my second project.

It became official! Project 2 was in the making! It was made up of three musicians: myself on the drums, Katie Lethin on the violin, and Janelle Gleason on the keyboard. They were both on board right away! Trying to make schedules work was one of the hardest parts (and that wasn't even *that* hard). All three of us only had one day in common that would work in the month I was wanting to record. After narrowing a day down, I now had to narrow a studio down that would also have this day available. So began the hunt for a studio!

I had been to quite a few places. I knew inside of me that I would know right away if said studio was the right one or not. A couple of the places seemed great, but I just didn't have that "a-ha!" moment. I had scheduled an appointment with another studio (it was probably the sixth studio that I saw up to that point). I had an audio recorded clip on my phone from the musicians practicing. I showed the engineer the clip, and that is when I knew he was the one to produce this project! I turned it on, and he closed his eyes and began moving his head to the beat of the music, along with a smile on his face. I thought to myself, "This is it. This guy loves what he does." I didn't want to just settle for someone educated. I wanted to get an engineer that loved music and loved what he did. It just so happened to be a bonus that this guy was smart!

Enough practice time with the music team? Check! A day that works for all of us? Check! Reservations for the recording studio? Check!

Before we knew it, it was studio day! We recorded 16 songs and put in a *long* six-hour day. What was even more amazing was that we all still loved each other afterwards (well, I hope we all did). I am *so* thankful that those two girls did this project with me. My engineer called me once the master copy was ready. I went back to the studio to pick it up, and he showed me several different sections. I seriously couldn't believe it! It sounded great! My favorite part of the whole CD is going into the chorus of "How Great Thou Art" and how the drums build up and do this huge crescendo! That captures the title of the project, *Music From The Heart*, to a "T."

In addition to producing these two projects, I have also somehow managed to get my Master's degree in Professional Counseling. I am still in awe when I step back and view these last two years at Corban University. The training that I have been given has been top notch! I also was able to do my clinical internship for a year at the Washington County Jail in Hillsboro, Oregon. Both of these locations have provided me with an excellent foundation in entering the Clinical Mental Health Profession.

In an earlier chapter, I talked about wanting to climb my Mt. Everest—Multnomah Falls. As I am writing this, I am still "flying higher than a kite." Just over 24 hours ago, I reached the top of Multnomah Falls! I decided that I wanted to try it one more time this year before the weather got too bad. I was determined! I picked up one of my friends and we started to climb. We started at the base of the mountain (as most people do). Two hours and 40 breaks (no exaggeration) later we looked out and we were level with the top of Multnomah Falls! I pulled out my bucket list and crossed it off! It feels great to accomplish another dream!

Lastly, on top of all of these "very small" projects, I also decided to write a book—this book to be precise. Needless to say, 2016 was definitely a productive year for me. It just goes to say that with perseverance, dedication, and hard work, you can chase after your dreams. But not only chase, you can also fulfill them, even more so when you invite God to be involved.

CONCLUDING THOUGHTS

I didn't think that I would have enough personal stories and information to fill the pages of a book. However, when I started to write, I found that I was not at a loss for stories. And I am sure that many of you can relate as well. There are many things that happen in our life that go unnoticed. We don't want people to see that we are in pain over something that may appear "frivolous" to other people. So we do our best to shove it into some dark corner in our heart and try to forget about it. But the sad thing is that it is still there. Just because we ignore pain doesn't mean that it will go away. In fact, the more we ignore pain, the harder it becomes to deal with it.

Obviously, I am not suggesting that we get a bull horn and drive through town announcing to anyone and everyone what we are dealing with. However, I think having that one person that truly understands can go a long way. Unfortunately, there are some who haven't even had the privilege of having that one person. If you fall into that category, I am truly sorry. The Bible encourages us to help our neighbors.

> Carry each other's burdens, and in this way you will fulfill the law of Christ.
>
> —Galatians 6:2

As hard as life my get, I want to encourage you to not waste your pain. I know, I know, when in crisis, helping someone else out can be far from our mind. Instead of hiding it and keeping it all bottled up, use it to help strengthen others, and in turn that could possibly help strengthen you. After all, we aren't doing this journey called life by ourselves. We have our brothers and sisters to help carry us in the seasons when life hurts.

Printed in the United States
By Bookmasters